Praise for

A Bridge to Buddhist-Christian Dialogue

"This new edition of Yagi's work significantly opens a new gateway for Buddhist-Christian dialogue, particularly through his profound concept of the Front-Structure, where all beings are understood as poles in dynamic relationality. I plan to use this text in both my Christian theology and Buddhism courses, as it offers an invaluable resource for students exploring interreligious thought."

—**Kunihiko Terasawa**, Associate Professor of Religion, Wartburg College

"It is still uncommon for a Japanese religion/theology scholar's work to be translated and featured in the West. This is why this revised republication of eminent interreligious studies scholar Leonard Swidler's translation of Seiichi Yagi's important work is a very welcome event and a rare treat! Yagi is, without doubt, one of the most eminent Japanese scholars working on interreligious dialogue and understanding, among other fields that include the New Testament. This important book offers unique contributions not only to Buddhist-Christian dialogue but to the wider field of interreligious conversations. It does that particularly through Yagi's concept of the 'Front-Structure' which provides an ingenious way to go beyond the typical Western substance-based paradigm of individual existence and suggests a conceptual model that is more relational and dynamic. This results in building a crucially important 'bridge' that leads to a deeper understanding and appreciation of both Buddhism and Christianity."

—**Julius-Kei Kato**, Professor of Religious Studies, King's College at Western University

"Like the Front-Structure theme of this book, two pillars of the religious dialogue community—one a Japanese Protestant Christian, the other a Wisconsin-bred Catholic theologian—combine to bridge the gap between a traditional understanding of Buddhist emptiness and Christianity's belief in God. With Leonard Swidler's insights into Seiichi Yagi's *A Bridge to Buddhist to Christian Thinking* and Yagi's call for a transcendence of interrelatedness, we have agreement on a method for connecting the dots between the ultimate modalities of both religions. This book builds on Swidler's longstanding call for a common language of unity capable of lifting all faiths."

—**John Tate**, Author and Independent Researcher

A BRIDGE TO BUDDHIST-CHRISTIAN DIALOGUE

Seiichi Yagi

and

Leonard Swidler

IPUB CLOUD INTERNATIONAL
POUGHKEEPSIE, NEW YORK

Published in the United States by
iPub Cloud International
Poughkeepsie, New York 12603
www.ipubcloud.org

Cover art by: Tori Abuschinow
Cover design by: Luis F. Ramos
Interior design by: Luis F. Ramos

Library of Congress Control Number: 2025943324

ISBN (paperback): 978-1-948575-95-9
ISBN (ebook): 978-1-948575-96-9

Table of Contents

PART ONE: A BRIDGE FROM BUDDHIST TO CHRISTIAN THINKING

PART TWO: A JERUSALEM-TOKYO BRIDGE

On the Occasion of the Republication of Front-Structure

The theory of "Front-Structure" has evolved significantly since *A Bridge to Buddhist-Christian Dialogue* was first published thirty-seven years ago. A brief summary of this development is as follows:

- The individual is not a substance but rather a pole within a field of action.
- The field is the foundation of the pole, and the pole expresses the field.
- The relationship between poles is the front-reciprocity and assimilation, forming an integrated body (coexistence).

For example, within the field of gravity, the celestial bodies orbiting the sun form an integrated system we call the solar system, and their movement reflects the structure of the gravitational field.

Now, there exists a transcendent field in which individuals, as poles, form an integrated body. For instance, in 1 Corinthians 12, Paul describes the church as "the body of Christ," (see 1 Cor 12-14, 27) indicating that within the transcendent field of action called "Christ," each believer becomes a pole, collectively forming an integrated body. Paul also states, "Christ dwells within me," (Gal 2:20) implying that Christ lives within believers, and their lives express Christ's work.

If we construct a field theory centered on this perspective, the overall structure closely aligns with the prologue of the Gospel of John (John 1:1-5). I will briefly outline the results of this development in accordance with this framework.

At its core is the Logos—a transcendent field that realizes the "principle of integration," the field of integrative action. However, integration is a fundamental form rather than the ultimate reality. The ultimate transcendence is not "being" itself but the "field of creative emptiness," within which being and non-being, life and death, arise.

Thus, the field of integrative action exists within and overlaps with the "field of creative emptiness," mediating and expressing this ultimate field. In doing so, it enables individuals to function as poles and move toward coexistence.

In the biological world, concepts such as competition for survival, survival of the fittest, and natural selection are often emphasized. However, these represent only one aspect of biological life. In reality, life has developed over four billion years, forming a natural world in which millions of species coexist. The destruction of this coexistence is caused by human beings.

Everything that exists is subject to the integrative action of transcendence. The resulting integrated bodies take various forms, such as atoms and solar systems, with living organisms among the most representative. The integration of the world and humanity—coexistence—embodies the Logos, which both signifies the meaning of life and serves as its guiding light.

Human beings, who have emerged through the function of integrative action, are beings that express this integration; Jesus serves as the prime example. Thus, while the Gospel of John identifies the Logos with Jesus as the incarnation of God, Jesus, as a historical figure, was one of those who expressed the Logos—a representative of transcendence but not transcendence itself.

How, then, did this identification come to be? My interpretation follows.

Jesus's disciples did not fully understand who and what he was. After his death, however, they became aware that the "kingdom of God" (transcendent integrative action), about which Jesus preached, was working within them (1 Cor 15:1-8; Gal 2:20).

A precedent for such an interpretation can be found in the gospels. After John the Baptist's death, when Jesus began a ministry grew beyond John's, many explained his powers as evidence that John the Baptist has been raised from the dead and was working through him (Mark 6:14; Matt 14:1-2; Luke 9:7-9).

Since such an interpretation already existed at the time, it is not surprising that after Jesus's death, his disciples—who recognized the working of the "kingdom of God" within themselves—understood this as the work of the resurrected and spiritualized Jesus. In this way, the identification of the resurrected Jesus with transcendent integration was established.

Clarifying the Relationship Between Christianity and Buddhism

When understood in this way, the correspondence between Christianity and Buddhism becomes clear. Consider the following parallels:

Christianity	**Buddhism**
God / Logos	The Dharma-nature and the Dharma-body Dharmakāya
Christ	Subtle body of limitless form of Amida Buddha Saṃbhogakāya
Jesus	Gautama Buddha *Nirmāṇakāya*

However, in practical terms, integrative action is not always strong enough to inevitably create integrated bodies. There are also forces that disrupt biological integration, such as natural disasters. The action of creative emptiness does not necessarily operate through integrative action. At this point, traditional Christian theology introduces the concept of *Deus absconditus*—the hidden God.

Issues in Language

Front-Structure and integration cannot be fully described in univocal language. This is because the pole exists in relation to others—it is itself through its relationships. In other words, the absolutization of univocal language destroys integration.

Univocal language, in practical terms, manifests as laws and morality. In cognition, it is used for classification, generalization, causal relationships, and means-end reasoning. This kind of language facilitates utility, control, and domination, ultimately reducing integration to uniformity and leading to its destruction.

Thus, conversion (metanoia) and enlightenment demand liberation from the dominance of univocal language. In Paul's case, this is expressed as, "The letter kills, but the Spirit gives life" (2 Cor 3:6). In Zen Buddhism, this is conveyed by the phrase "no reliance on words and letters" (不立文字).

Acknowledgment for the Republication

Regarding this republication, I would like to express my heartfelt gratitude to Professor Leonard Swidler, the translator of this book, as well as to his student, Associate Professor Kunihiko Terasawa of Wartburg College, who not only facilitated communication between Professor Swidler and me but also carefully translated my new statement for this edition.

Seiichi Yagi
February 20, 2025

Preface by Seiichi Yagi

The world is becoming increasingly interconnected, the contact between peoples is growing closer, and the awareness of the relativity of traditions is becoming clearer. Thus, it is not surprising that in Europe, the United States, and Japan, Christians and Buddhists are increasingly engaging with one another, not because Christians view Buddhism as a hindrance to their mission, but because they now see it as a dialogue partner.

For Christians in Japan, this concerns their very destiny. In this land, they do not encounter Buddhism merely as a doctrine, but as something lived by their contemporaries—by Buddhists who embody it. When Christians, in dialogue with them, recognize a profound relatedness that challenges the absolute claim of Christianity, they are compelled to ask what this relatedness is, where it comes from, and what it means for the Christian faith.

My essay is an attempt to respond to these questions through the lens of the concept of the "Front-Structure." Naturally, such a brief treatment cannot present a fully developed argument. Instead, this work offers a preliminary sketch—a study in the form of an outline—for a broader conceptual system. That system has emerged from dialogue with Buddhism and from efforts to articulate an adequate framework within that dialogue (including Front-Structure, integration, and related ideas).

I wish to express my heartfelt gratitude, first of all, to Professor Theo Sundermeier, co-editor of the German series *Ökumenische Existenz heute*, within which my essay originally appeared under the title *Die Front-Struktur als Brücke vom buddhistischen zum christlichen Denken* (Munich: Chr. Kaiser Verlag, 1988). It was he who encouraged me to write it.

I am also deeply pleased to address American readers through this English translation of my small book, which was written for those who recognize the necessity of interfaith dialogue and the transformation of religion through such dialogue. For religion must be always interpreted anew in light of the needs arising from new cultural and religious contexts. Now more than ever, a radical renewal of religion is necessary to foster mutual understanding among us human beings, who must live together on our increasingly small planet.

I am especially grateful that this book is being published in the United States, where many are open and receptive to non-Western traditions and alternative ways of thinking—traditions that are proving to be constitutive of our shared cultural-religious future.

Finally, I wish to express my heartfelt thanks to Professor Leonard Swidler, the translator of this book, who—quite unexpectedly—undertook the work of translation and, in doing so, encouraged and furthered international dialogue.

Tokyo, January, 1989
Seiichi Yagi

Preface by Leonard Swidler

In the latter half of 1988, Seiichi Yagi's small book on the Front-Structure as a Bridge from Buddhist to Christian Thinking appeared in German. That fall, I was on sabbatical leave, living in Tübingen, Germany, nestled peacefully between the Swabian Alb and the Black Forest. Initially, I began reading Yagi's little book out of general curiosity—but I soon found myself having an "aha!" experience. In a sense, I already knew everything Yagi was writing about, but I had never before seen it laid out so clearly and accessibly, in concepts and language with which I felt completely at home. So I immediately sat down and wrote him to ask about translating the book into English—fortunately for me he had written it originally in German rather than Japanese. He responded that he would be pleased to have it translated and so, I undertook the translation.

As I began thinking about writing an introduction for the American edition, I realized that although I took to the book "like a duck to water," not all Western readers would share my background in interreligious dialogue—particularly with Buddhism. I therefore thought it would be helpful to prepare the ground for Seiichi Yagi's bridge. That is what I attempt to do in my introductory essay.

After some brief reflections on interreligious dialogue in general, I discuss in more detail eleven major topics that have been central to the ongoing Buddhist-Christian dialogue. I then turn to Japan, where Seiichi Yagi is from, and offer a brief overview of the development of Buddhism there—along with a shorter discussion of Christianity in Japan. Finally, I examine Yagi himself: his role in Japanese religious life, the development of his thought, and, specifically, the focus of this book.

Readers who are already familiar with the current state of Buddhist-Christian dialogue may wish to proceed directly to Chapters IV and V, where I discuss Yagi and his thought in greater depth.

This is the first English-language book in which Seiichi Yagi appears as more than a contributing author. It clearly will not be his last. His books in Japanese have sold hundreds of thousands of copies—mostly to non-Christians, despite the fact that he is a Protestant Christian and a New Testament scholar. His early works focused exclusively on

Christianity and the New Testament, but in recent years he has shifted toward a profound dialogue between Buddhist and Christian thought—and life. It is here that Yagi has been at his most creative, as often happens in moments of deep intellectual and spiritual cross-pollination.

Yagi's knowledge of the New Testament and of contemporary scholarship is both profound and subtle. Remarkably, the same is also true of his understanding of Buddhist teaching and thought. In this book, we are presented with the fruit of a deep dialogue between Buddhist and Christian thought—one that takes place within the mind of the author himself. What is most valuable is his ability to share the results of that dialogue in such clear and articulate language.

The subject of this dialogue is neither simple nor superficial; it is complex and profound, and thus demands close reading. Yet that effort is richly rewarded, as language that once confused and conceptualizations that once seemed obscure are made clear and understandable.

Philadelphia, January, 1989
Leonard Swidler

PART ONE

A Bridge from Buddhist to Christian Thinking

The Front-Structure

by

Seiichi Yagi

Front-Structure and Buddhist Thinking

Front-Structure

What is sunyata?[1] Our starting point is an essay by Keiji Nishitani.[2] It begins with the following very impressive explanation for sunyata: When two rooms, A and B, are divided by a wall (W), as in sketch number one below, the wall (W) is an indispensable component of both rooms, since it is not possible to have a room without the walls.

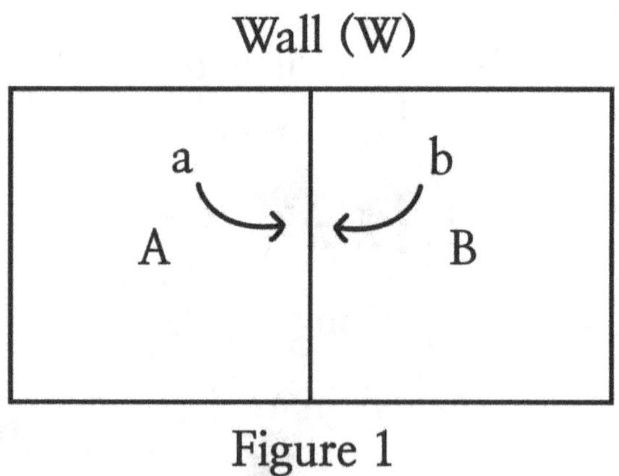

Figure 1

When, however, in room B one sees the surface of wall W which is in room B, that is, the surface "b," this "b," although a component of B, is to be viewed as the expression of the adjoining room A since the surface "b" manifests the "existence" (Dasein) of A. When in room B one sees the surface of the wall "b," then "b" is that by which room A projects itself into room B, indeed not as A or "a," but rather as "b," namely, as a part of B.

This relationship can be discovered everywhere. Imagine a tree. The leaves of the tree form carbohydrates from carbon dioxide and water by using the energy of the sunlight. Thus, the carbohydrates become a constitutive part of the tree. One can say that the energy of the sunlight has projected itself into the tree as the energy of the carbohydrates.

If we apply this way of viewing things to other matters, we will conclude the following: no component of myself, no constitutive part of myself is something that I alone have brought forth from myself. From this we can define the Buddhist technical term Muge ("in one another without hindrance") in the following manner: That which is found outside of me is transformed into a constitutive part of me in that what now belongs to me still continues to remain a part of that which is outside of me. The nature, the openness, of our reality, that is, that by which this in one another becomes possible, it called sunyata. In other words, if an existing being were so structured that the coming into it of another existing being were not allowed, if existing beings simply excluded each other, then there would be no sunyata. Sunyata, then, means that no existing being is composed simply and exclusively of the constitutive parts which belong to itself alone.

Since with this explanation of the essence of sunyata and Muge Nishitani has clearly hit the mark, we need almost no further explanations. Nevertheless, we will attempt to develop his interpretation further because we wish to make it our starting point.

Before we go along this path, however, let us return once again to Figure 1 in order to correct something in it. For among our readers some could discover a difficulty in the statement that "b" is the expression of A. They might think that "b" is from the beginning a component of B, that therefore "b" is not necessarily an expression of A. This reflection is completely justified. For "b" would exist as "b" if the room B had no adjoining room A.

Let us think that through once again. We see "b" not directly as the expression of A, but rather we understand "b" first of all as the surface of the wall (W), which is found in room B. Then we can say that this surface of W, while it remains the surface of W, at the same time is a constitutive part, a component of B.

In this we can also call attention to the fact that the wall (W) does not function as wall—that is, is not the wall—until it takes on this position. If it were separated from the room and set aside, then it would merely be a rectangular board, whatever it may be made out of. The board first becomes a wall when it divides a space into two rooms, for a room needs the wall in order to be a room. The walls and the room condition each other. It is not so that the one calls forth the other. This mutual conditioning in Buddhism is called *Soe Sogan*[3], "mutual dependence and relatedness." This concept is important in order to understand Buddhism. In our example the walls and the room condition each other.

I will now introduce a further concept. Let us call b, namely, the surface of the wall in room B, the Front of the wall (W). Then of course the surface "a" is the other Front of W. The Front is that in which we encounter the other. The Front "a" belongs to A and expresses A, so that contact with the Front of A is an encounter with A itself. The Front is, however, also the border. It can be hostile. It can move and force its way into the area of the other and destroy it. This hostility of a Front must always be borne in mind. If we thus define Front, then "a" in figure number one is the Front of the wall which has become a component of A, while b similarly is the Front of the wall which has become a constitutive part of B. The wall (W) separates and joins A and B because their Fronts "a" and "b" each are constitutive parts of A and B. When therefore the Front of one object, while it remains its Front, has become a constitutive part of another object, we call this structure a Front-Structure.[4] Stated more generally: it is the structure in which the Front of A, while remaining that Front, has become a constitutive part, a component of non-A. Then the Front "a" belongs 100 percent to A, while at the same time it belongs 100 percent to non-A. In this of course the viewpoint from which it belongs to A and the viewpoint from which it belongs to non-A are respectively different. Then this Front is the unity of A and non-A, or we can say: A and non-A are, as this Front, one and the same. This state of affairs would be expressed in Buddhist technical terminology as "A soku Non-A."[5] "Soku" therefore means "is/is not." This soku arises in the Front-Structure. There are various forms of Front-Structure, and correspondingly also of soku, which we later on will investigate more precisely.

Examples of Front-Structure

1. A house has a garden in which there are planted trees and in which flowers are blooming. Every plant in the garden is a part of nature, the Front of nature. We encounter nature in the trees and grasses in the garden. One says: "When you see a leaf fall from the branch, you know that Fall is there."

   On the other hand, the garden is also a part of the living area of a family. That is, the garden is the Front of nature which has become a part of a human living area. Human living stands in contrast to nature. However, the essence of the garden lies in the fact that it is the Front of nature which has become intermeshed in the family life. The plants grow in the garden and attract insects which disturb us. Thus, nature is not always perceived by us as friendly. Hence, we control the growth of the plants, destroy the damaging insects, in order to maintain the Front-Structure, which is the essence of the garden, but we do not totally eliminate nature from the garden, for that would annihilate the garden.

2. The Front-Structure also exists in the city. We are concerned about the beauty of our cities in that we, for example, try to harmonize the heights and colors of the buildings and refrain from a ruthless spread of advertisements, and the like. In this, of course, a tasteless uniformity is to be avoided and a harmony should be developed instead. Now, the outer wall of the building is a part of the city, therefore, a component of the public space. The special characteristic of the outer wall of the building in the city lies in the fact that the private facade at the same time takes on a public significance. We can always see at the dividing line between the private and the public that the Front of the private life is a component of public life.

In both of these examples the Front-Structure is static. Therefore, in the next examples a dynamic process will be outlined.

This next example may sound somewhat strange, but nevertheless something essential and important will be illustrated by it. In the womb the child is connected with the placenta by means of the umbilical cord. Thereby the child receives everything it needs from the mother. We ask now whether the nourishment which the umbilical cord draws from the mother into the child is a part of the child or of the mother. Here the univocal alternative "either-or" does not fit. Everything which flows from the mother into the child is the Front of the mother, which has become a component of the child. In this case the Front-Structure shows forth the essential relationship between the mother and the child in the womb. The child lives because it transforms the Front of the mother into its own component part. Here is the essence of the life activity of the embryo.

We, therefore, call this activity by which a being transforms the Front of another being into its own component part "Front-Appropriation." The living being maintains through this "Front-Appropriation" its "Front-Structure," and thereby also its life. Seen from the side of the mother, she gives to the child in her body her own Front through the umbilical cord. We can call this activity of the mother "Front-Gift." "Front-Gift" and "Front-Appropriation" in many cases go hand in hand. Mother and child live through it. The relationship between the mother and the child in her body consists in giving and taking. Giving and taking occur through the Front-Gift and Front-Appropriation.

It is interesting to see that an individual or a community does not itself consume all that it produces, but gives some of it to others as its Front, so that the exchange of the Fronts produces the effect that they live *together*. An interesting instance of this is found in the matrimonial system, through which the co-existence of families is enabled. The incest taboo, which necessitates the exchange of women, is, according to Levi-Strauss, the negative side of the necessity of Front-Exchange. This is not unlike the exchange of meson between elemental particles, by which they are bound together.

Front-Expansion

The process of appropriation can also be seen in the tree example. When we call something a tree, we are referring to an object with roots, trunk, branches and leaves. That is, we think of a tree in that we separate it from other things. This takes place on the basis of our habit of language. When we speak, a sentence consists of a subject and predicate. When we state the subject, we state it in that we separate it from other objects. With the word "tree" we think of an object which is nothing other than a tree. Consequently, we assume almost unavoidably that a tree is a tree from out of itself, that it is nothing other than a tree, that is, that there is nothing in it which does not belong exclusively to the tree. However, if we look a little more closely, it becomes clear that the existence of a tree at the same time includes the fact that there is also sunlight, air, water, earth, and the whole history of the living being. The existence of the sun and the earth literally means the existence of the whole cosmos. Thus, the existence of a tree includes the existence of the whole cosmos. We recall here a word by Dogen (1200–1253), a Japanese Zen master of the Kamakura: "When the old plum tree blooms, the whole world is in its blossoms."[6] Here we notice that the tree maintains itself in that it takes up into itself water and carbon dioxide and from that produces carbohydrates by applying the energy of sunlight. It maintains itself, therefore, by transforming the Fronts of other things into its own constituent parts, that is, through Front-Appropriation.

Almost everywhere, we find the Front-Giving and Front-Appropriation in living beings. Take for example the relationship between the heart and the lungs: the heart pumps the blood into all parts of the body so that we can view the blood streaming from the heart and its pulse beat as the Fronts of the heart. The condition of the heart can be known by the pulse beat. Thus, the blood which flows in the lungs is the Front of the heart, but it is at the same time a part of the activity of the lungs themselves. Since the function of the lungs consists in the exchange of gas, the flowing of the blood in the lungs belongs to the activity of the lungs themselves. In our terminology: the Front of the heart is a constituent part of the lungs. Here we see in the relationship between the heart and the lungs the Front-Giving and the Front-Appropriation which constitutes the essence of the relationship between the two.

We notice: the blood, which is pumped by the heart into all parts of the body, is the Front of the heart. Whatever the medical definition might be, a living heart is not an object separated from the arteries. In the body the heart without arteries is unthinkable, and indeed there are even arteries in the heart itself. We must see the entire system of arteries as the Front of the heart, just as the peripheral nerves are the Front of the brain. That does not mean, however, that the entire system of arteries is called the heart. Our view is the following: the Front of the heart expands itself into all parts of the body. We perceive here the expansion of the Front of the heart. We see in this case that the pulse beat is strongest near the heart and that it becomes ever weaker the farther away the arteries are from the heart. Therefore, in Front-Expansion one can speak of strengths and weaknesses in the power of expression of the Front. In our case the arteries nearest the heart express the heart most strongly, while the expansion of the Front in the capillary system is the greatest.

Shishio Nakamura (1898–1953) in his book, *The Philosophical Understanding of Christianity,* coined the concept of the "nebula structure,"[7] like a patch of fog. This structure is seen in a nebula which in its center is quite obvious and thick, but which expands into infinity, in that it becomes less obvious and ever thinner. According to Nakamura, sin, for example, has this structure. It is located in the center of the person and expands its effects to its periphery, so that it shows itself in facial expressions and conduct.

In fact, this concept is much more widely applicable than Nakamura believed. In order to interpret it according to our own conceptualization, we will call the nebula structure "Front-Expansion." The Front expands itself like the patch of fog. More generally spoken, the whole effect of the distortion which a being causes in a "field of force" is to be viewed as the Front of the being.

When we see a distant star in the night sky, we can still know something about it, for the radiation of that star reaches us. That means, however, that the Front (the optical Front) of a star is here on the earth. That we here can observe an infinite number of stars means that the Front of an infinite number of stars concentrate on this point on the earth where we observe them. We encounter the stars in their optical Fronts on the earth and gather much information about them. The following is thinkable: If a star is extinguished even millions of years ago, its light continues still to reach the earth, as the words of Jesus reach us and continue to address us although he himself died 2,000 years ago. In the case of the extinguished star we encounter the star here and now as it was several million years ago.

What is decisively important in this is the following: When we grasp the optic Front of a star, that is, when we see it, we do not grasp a periphery of the star which has been separated from it. That we grasp the optical Front of the star means much more that we see the star itself, that we encounter the star itself in its Front (otherwise we did not encounter it at all). That means, however, that the star is there in its Front. It is there as a whole. At every point of the earth there come together the rays of the sun which radiate out from all parts of the sun which are turned toward the earth. Therefore, we see the sun here as a whole, we do not see a limited part of it. The Front of all parts of the sun gather together at every point on the earth so that a tiny drop of water mirrors the entire sun in itself. We can analogically say further that the Front of all organs concentrate at every point of our body so that we can know the condition of our entire body from the condition of one part of our body. In other words, one part of our body reflects back the health condition of the entire body. That is possible because the Fronts of one organ expand themselves like a nebula so that the fronts of all organs concentrate on every point of our body as something which has been appropriated by this part of the body—only that the manner of concentration is different according to each location. The nature of our body allows that—an important recognition of the nature of sunyata.

Important Examples of Front-Structure

Now that we have become familiar with several easily understood examples of Front-Structure, let us reflect on several further important examples.

A. We ascertain the Front-Structure in *perception*. One says: I see a tree. However, that does not mean that I first am there and that separate from me there is an "object," a tree, and afterwards I and the tree come into contact, so that only then the perception takes place. For by such a construction the existence of the tree must be posited independent of the perception—which is absurd. Or is it? If we hold reason and material to be two substances, as Descartes did, then it cannot be explained how two substances come into a relationship to each other. Rather: In our case my perception is in reality the appropriated optical Front of the tree. That is first of all clear for the objectifying manner of observation. The optical stimulus's transfer in the nerves to the brain, the transformed Front of the tree, is at once the activity of the nerves themselves; that is, the Front of the tree which has been appropriated by the nerves.

We can now try a small experiment: If we touch, for example, a table with a finger and in the process, move the finger or tap on the table with it, we feel something which is outside of the finger. However, when we do not move the finger on the table, we feel the condition of our own, pressed and cooled finger. That is then not the perception of an object. But the sensation itself is one. There are not two separate sensations, one of the object and one of the condition of one's own finger, such that the sensation of touching were a complex of both sensations. Rather, we articulate a simple sensation in two polar directions, outwardly and inwardly, in such a way that the sensation itself indicates that it comes from the outside and at the same time it indicates the inner condition. If we take, then, the sense of touch of the moving finger to be the transformed Front of an object, we see that it precisely thereby provides information about the outside world because the sense of touch is the Front of the object appropriated by my senses. In this, of course, it must be noted that with the help of the sense of touch the sensation itself is oriented in two polar directions—toward the object and toward the subject.

This experiment, however, is difficult to carry with the sense of sight. That is because the sense of sight is so very much bound up with our "objective" knowledge with the result that we are hardly ever aware of the condition of our own eyes in the sensation of seeing. However, the "after-image," the visual sensation which remains for a brief time after we have closed our eyes—shows that even the sense of sight presents the condition of the sense organ since it is no longer the perception of a there existing "object," although content wise it is identical with it. From this we can see that in order to intuitively experience the Front-Structure we must free ourselves from objectifying thinking. This is what we wish to pursue in the following chapter. Here it only needs to be remarked that in the "immediate experience"[8] we become aware that even the sensation of sight both presents the outside world (as object) and at the same time is the inside mental activity of the "subject."

B. Our body, as we know, is made up of matter, and every process of its living activity is a process of material reactions. Nevertheless, we cannot simply identify our *bodies* with matter—in any case, not with matter as it is objectively grasped. Such a naive identification would be as if one were to identify a painting, for example, by Rouault with a patch of paint because both of them consist of form and color. The fundamental recognition that the body is more than the sum of its matter is a fundamental axiom of modern humanistic sciences. We recognize, as was already mentioned, that every process of the living activity of a body is a process of matter. That means, however, that our body is the Front of the material world. More precisely said, from the fact that we maintain our life through eating and drinking we perceive that our body consists of the Fronts of the world which have been transformed into the constituent parts of our body. For example, the material behavior of the oxygen in our body is at the same time a part of our living activity itself. All material processes of our body have as their meaning the maintenance of life. We are a part of the world, but in such a way that the Fronts of matter appropriated into our bodies form our personal existence.

We can see this from yet another viewpoint: there is no Ego without the body. Nevertheless, the Ego from a certain perspective can stand in opposition to the body. That is shown in linguistic expressions like: "I use my body" or "I move my hands and feet," and so forth. From this point of view the body is the instrument of the Ego which acts in the outer world through the body. In this sense my body is my Front which belongs to the world. My body exists, therefore, because it is at once the Front of the world to me and, at the same time my Front in the world. Thus, my bodily movement, my face, are expressions of me.

That means, however, we encounter the world in, by, and through our body. We could probably from this perspective interpret in our manner the Heideggerian concept "to be-in-the-world." However, we are not merely in the world. My body is the Front of the world, which constitutes me, but it is also my Front in the world, which belongs to the world. Here we see the basis on which we can act at all in the world, can express ourselves in the world. If, therefore, in the Front-Appropriation a disturbance takes place, I and the world could find ourselves in a hostile relationship to each other. For example, I can go for a walk. I am using then the gravity of the earth. The gravity binds me to the earth, but I transform it into the condition whereby I can walk. I could not walk if there were no gravity. This activity of transforming the forces of the world into the conditions of my own existence or behavior, however, can be reckoned as the Front-Appropriation in a wider sense. The fact that I cannot walk when, for example, I have a muscular disorder, shows that the very being of our body lies in the Front-Structure.

C. The Front-Structure is found not only in the relationship of the living being to its surrounding or outer world, but also in the relationship of living beings to one another. The most illustrative example is the structure of the ecosystem, that is, the relationship between animals, plants and bacteria.

I once had a goldfish. I washed one surface of the cubic goldfish bowl clean and allowed water plants to grow on the other surfaces. Thus, the goldfish bowl became a small space in which animal, plant and bacteria lived together. The excretions of the fish were decomposed by the bacteria and the plants were fertilized with it. Thus, the plants purified the water and provided the water with oxygen through photosynthesis. In this manner the water was only slightly contaminated so that I needed to change the water just once a month. In this way my goldfish lived almost twelve years. There are similar relationships between animals, plants, and bacteria in nature. Here we see again a type of Front-Structure in a wider sense, although in this case the Front of a living being which is "appropriated" by other living beings, is separated from its center and is alienated from it. This form of Front-Appropriation or Front-Exchange is thus not representative. Nevertheless, even here the Front-Structure exhibits the condition for mutual living.

D. We will provide one more example of the Front-Giving and the Front-Appropriation in order then to proceed to our central theme. From the beginning we wished to investigate language, and specifically language as address. The word, or more generally spoken, *language*, is the Front of a person. When a person addresses me, I encounter her in her address. The word which she speaks is her Front. And in her Front, I encounter the person herself, just as I see the star itself when I see a star, although I really only grasp an optical Front here on the earth. In the address, if I encounter the addressing person herself, then the addressing person is *within* the Front grasped as address, and has been appropriated by me—that is, is within me. As the voice of the one addressing is already in me as the one appropriated by me, so also is the word of a person perceived as an address in me, and here the person herself is present.

What is the difference between the voice of a person and a mere physical tone? The voice is, physically described, the waves of the air. The voice, however, is also that by which I encounter the person who speaks to me, although the voice contains nothing special physically or physiologically beyond the mere tone. Nevertheless, the voice of a person calls forth a reaction in the one hearing, as can be observed in a baby which hears the voice of its mother. The voice calls forth the reaction. The reaction is something original, although through secondary experiences it is strengthened or weakened. The voice, in which the one speaking is present when it is heard by me, is in me as that which has been appropriated by me. Therefore, it can work in me: it calls forth my reaction.

Now, what is the reaction? Stimulus and reaction are not two different things. The stimulus is constitutive for the reaction. The reaction reflects the stimulus. In this regard the Front of the one stimulating has become a moment of the reaction itself in the one reacting. When I respond to an address I transform the address into the constitutive condition through which the response happens if the response also takes place as a free act. The address penetrates into the very center of my personality and, as a factor of my personality, still expresses *in me* the addressing person. Here again we see a type of Front-Structure.

E. The telephone is a useful instrument. Today we all use it. The receiver mechanically reproduces the voice of the one who addresses me on the telephone—which had already transformed the voice into an electric signal (so that we speak of a Front-Transformation). Nevertheless, I encounter in fact the one who is on the telephone. Without the Front-Expansion that would be unthinkable. I encounter the one who addresses me in the voice and words which are perceived as an address. The person is present there. Through the Front of the person which has been appropriated by me, this person is in me—in a certain sense is one with me—but of course not in such a manner that, for example, a part of the person would be substantially transported into me. In this case there is nothing substantial in the Front. Nevertheless, I encounter the person in it.

This shows how a unity between persons comes into existence. The unity is not a substantial melding together. Still, it is important that in the expanded Front which has been appropriated by me, the encounter with the person takes place, and thereby the unity with the person is present. Here there is no exchange of substances, as, for example, with the relationship between the mother and the not-yet-born child. Nevertheless, we can speak of the unity of the persons in this Front-Structure, all the more since the Front represents the whole person and it is in it that the encounter takes place. There are, then, *two different forms of the Front-Structure* (the third type, "field-type" will be discussed below in Chapter III): One is, so to speak, the *substantial type*, in which something substantial is given and appropriated; the other is the wave type, in which the Front can be compared to a wave which stimulates an existing being and calls forth from it a reaction or resonance which reflects the stimulation without any substantial Front-Exchange: For example, in the resonance the one "hearing" appropriates the wave of the one sending, or, transforms the wave of the one sending into its own vibration. That is the wave-type of Front-Appropriation. However, with persons the reaction, or "resonance," is not merely mechanical, but is freely undertaken.

Now, in our connection what does "to understand" mean? The language which I speak is my own language. On the other hand, my language is not mine alone. It is something common to all. I affect other persons in that I address them in our common language, and vice versa. Thus, on the one hand the language belongs to me. It is my mental property. However, on the other hand, it is the Front of the other. None of the words which I use have been created by me. Their content, use, have been historically and socially specified. The fact that I know and use a word means that other persons have existed before me. The fact that I understand the word of another person means that it has become my own word or has become a constitutive part of my mental activity. Because, however, it remains the Front of the other person, I also encounter in this word the one speaking to me. The other person penetrates into me with his word; he has an effect on me. That I understand means that his Front has become a constitutive part of my thinking. Through such an understanding the other person can have an effect on me and call forth my response. In general, understanding means that the word of the other person, while remaining the Front of the person, has been transformed into my own word. Understanding is the activity of this appropriation. Without an address my response would not exist, and it is in the response that my becoming myself is realized, as Martin Buber has shown. Thus, we also see the Front-Structure in the "I and thou" relationship.

It has been many times experimentally confirmed that the human being becomes human only in the continuous process of address and response. Human beings indeed are born with the capacity of speech, but this possibility will never become reality if they do not learn to speak and are not trained in it. That is also true in general for all human capacities. Just as the gasoline engine will not start of itself, so also human possibilities will not awaken of themselves. They must be awakened. We need the "starter." If Mozart had been born in a land without any music, he would not have composed any operas or symphonies. This is also true in our understanding of persons in their Front-Expansion: A person's very existence, but especially a person's address and action have an effect on others. They function as starters. They act as the initiator of the wave which calls forth the reaction—which reaction reflects in itself the initiator. This wave will be appropriated by the person who allows it to have an effect on him or her such that the wave becomes a constitutive part of him or her. It is on the basis of this state of affairs that learning and also education are possible. The starter has an effect on a person; then she begins to act on her own, spontaneously and in her own manner. In this case the wave of the sender arouses the spontaneous activity of the one awakened. Here we are dealing not with a mere mechanism, but with the spontaneity of a human being. And yet, the wakefulness reflects the outside influence so that we can perceive the Front-Structure in the reflection.

I have been especially strongly influenced by several thinkers. The words of Jesus have taken hold in my heart, but they remain the words of Jesus. His words, which are difficult to chew, let alone digest, have been constantly working on me and appear to have awakened in me that of which he spoke: They have activated and started my life-possibilities which previously had been dormant. Because of what they awakened in me, they showed me that the reality of Jesus is a possibility for every human being. Gradually I began in my own way to express what Jesus spoke about. But then I did not simply repeat his words, but rather expressed them with my own words. However, my words still continue to reflect his words. In any case, his words have become my words because his words awakened, activated, and brought to language my possibility. In that measure I can say that I have understood his words.

Dilthey, Heidegger, and Bultmann have grounded and developed their hermeneutics in the following manner: The living expression of the past discloses our own possibilities. We will try to state that with our own concepts: The cultural products of the past, or more generally, the total cultural traditions, are the Fronts of the past, which we can make constitutive parts of our present culture. Here there is the Front-Giving and the Front-Appropriation as well as the temporal Front-Structure. This Front-Structure is not static. We must activate the tradition. Otherwise it remains dead. To activate the tradition means to understand it and to transform it into a constitutive part of our present. In this the Front of the past is more or less transformed. When we read classical texts we can do so with the help of the historical method. If we understand them and make them components of our present, they will be transformed since they will be woven into a culture strange to them, that is, they will be set into another context. The same is also valid for the response to the address of contemporary human beings. In both cases through understanding and through interpretation the Front-Structure of each one becomes newly present. In our temporal-social existence everyone gives their Front to the other and takes it from the other. Without that, education is unthinkable. One could even say that without the Front-Giving and Front-Appropriation it is not possible for the human being to become human.

The Individual Existing Being as a Pole

The Front-Structure belongs to the essence of life. Our existence is not like an atom in the sense of the classical Atomists; it is not an existing being which is separate from all other existing beings and depends on itself or can exist out of itself. It is not a substance which simply and unchangedly remains, which allows no penetration of the other into itself, which excludes everything other than itself from itself and can protect its self-identity. Living means living in the Front-Structure which is maintained through the constant Front-Giving and Front-Appropriation, that is, through the Front-Exchange. In other words, in every "slice,"[9] in every part of me, I encounter the other, whose Front constitutes me. It is, of course, not the case that something alien, something completely other dwells in and is active in me. Then I would be a crazy person. Rather, in what belongs to me and is an authentic constitutive part of me, I nevertheless encounter the Front of the other—the other self. There is nothing which exclusively and entirely belongs to me. There is no pure "I."

Let us now look somewhat more closely at the relationship of the existing beings which are bound together with one another in the Front-Structure. The things which are bound together with one another in the Front-Structure relate to one another as two poles. Between poles one can of course draw a distinction, but they cannot be separated from one another. One pole needs the opposite pole in order to be a pole. Let us look at the example of the magnet. The magnet has two poles which we distinguish, but which we cannot separate from each other. If we cut a magnet into two pieces the result is two small magnets. There is no magnet which functions with a north pole alone. The north pole needs the south pole in order to function as north pole. The earth has two poles. Let us imagine a longitudinal circle of the earth: if we cut it through and the slice is looked at from the perspective of the North Pole, the slice is a Front of the South Pole. The opposite is true as well. The same must likewise be said of a magnetic field. In this sense the northern polar circle seen from the North Pole is the Front of the South Pole. This indicates the structure of the polar circle. There is no substance which in itself would be the Pole. That the northern polar circle seen from the North Pole constitutes the Front of the South Pole does not mean that there is a substance or material which is called "Front." It means that every slice of the northern polar circle is the Front of the South Pole, that it expresses the South Pole as the Front.

Because this situation illustrates the Front-Structure, we will look into it a little more carefully here: imagine a space which is divided by two figures a and b into four parts, that is, "ab'," "ab," "a'b," "a'b'," (Figure 2).

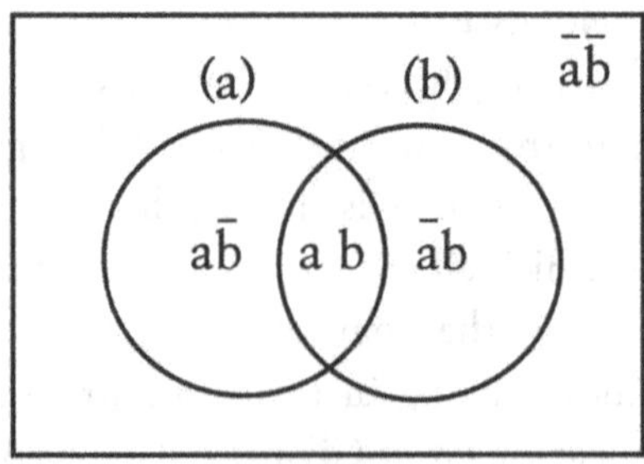

Figure 2

The part "ab" belongs now to both figures "a" and "b." The part "ab," being a part of "a," forms a part of "b." Do we see the Front-Structure here? No, that alone does not yet mean Front-Structure. The Front-Structure means that every point in "a" is the Front of "b," that it expresses "b" and that the Front of "b" is present in every point of "a," although the power of the expression of the Front is different corresponding to the position when the Fronts of "b" may also find themselves eventually only in a limited part of "a." The Front is not a substance. There is no substance which is in itself the Front. The Front is a relational concept. It is such that every slice, every surface, every part and every point of A is the Front of non-A, that A meets non-A in it, that the Front of non-A in A expresses non-A.

Indeed, there is, as mentioned, the substantial type of Front-Structure, but the substantiality as such is not the Front, but rather, something is called Front only insofar as it mediates an encounter. There are cases, however, in which the Front is cut off from the center: Pollen is the Front of a plant, sperm the Front of a man. These examples need to be investigated further.

The Front which is separated from the center and substitutes for it is important if we wish, for example, to see how language can substitute for reality.[10] Here we will limit ourselves to the typical Front-Structure in which the Front is bound to its center and expresses it. If two existing beings are found together in the Front-Structure, we can distinguish between them but we cannot separate them from each other. The Front-Structure is polar. Insofar as two persons coexist in the Front-Structure they are the poles. I am of course myself and no other person. I am not completely dependent on any person, but am self-supporting. That is true and to that extent self-identity is an indispensable moment of my being, without which I would not be a person. Nevertheless, when I am I, when I as I live, the Front-Giving and the Front-Appropriation arises. Persons live in a constant Front-Exchange. The person is polar. The independence of a person arises in the Front-Structure with others.

This fact is called *Muge* in Buddhism ("in one another without hindrance," or better, the "in one another of existing beings without hindrance"); this we are calling "Front-Structure." The "in one another of existing beings" means the negation of a pure self-identity or an absolute substantiality of the existing being. This negation is called "emptiness," "vacancy" or "openness," on whose account the "in-one-another" is possible. It is sunyata. In the following we will look further into what sunyata means.

The Distinction Between an Existing Being and an Individual

In order to clarify our subject, I wish to suggest a distinction between an individual[11] and an existing being. An individual is this or that thing. In our case it is above all an individual living being. With Aristotle, an individual was something separate from other things, indicated by "this," the primary substance which could be the subject of a sentence, but not its predicate. The word *individuum* is the Latin translation of the Greek word *atomon* by Cicero. It means "that which has no parts." For to *atomon*, the *individuum*, would be qualitatively other if it were broken into parts. In the Middle Ages the *individuum* was also something substantial, whose ontological specification was per *se esse*, "to exist through itself." It was not *ab se esse*, "to exist from itself," which would be God. Modern thought stands in this tradition and, although, as is known, Heidegger made a distinction between to be (*Sein*) and existing beings (*das Seiende*), in the European tradition the *individuum* was always taken to mean the existing being. On the other hand, let us recall here that in the New Testament the human being is sometimes referred to as the "non-existing being": "God, who makes the dead alive and calls into existence non-existing beings" (Rom 4:17b), or "God chose what is low and despised in the world, things that are not, to reduce to nothing things that are" (1 Cor 1:28a).[12]

In Buddhism, what has form is called *rupa*, in Japanese, *ke-u* (temporal existence). We can say that in Buddhism there is no word which strictly speaking has the same meaning as *individuum* (that which has no parts). According to it, the individual is temporal, scarcely unequivocally means the existing being. We wish to explain this with our concept of the Front-Structure. Our thesis is: Life has Front-Structure. In other words, the living being, or the so-called *individuum*, is a pole which cannot exist alone. Here, however, we understand by the concept of the existing being something which distinguishes itself from other beings in its self-identity which is limited on all sides, and is persistently there. Then the individual living being is in itself not an "existing being." When a fish is taken out of the water it quickly dies. The fish bought in the food store is, as a commercial item, doubtless an *individuum*, but it is no longer a true fish. (Indeed, one even sells parts of it.) When a plant is pulled out of the dirt it wilts. The human being likewise is in this respect no exception. A living being cannot continue to live where there is no longer a Front-Appropriation. It cannot exist alone. It ceases to live when it is taken out of relationship with others and is forced to exist for itself alone. In this sense the individual is in itself not an existing being. It is in itself much more a non-existing being.

We can picture an existing being as a closed rectangle (Figure 3a), for it has a specific form which is limited on all sides and is something self-identical. Then we will have to illustrate individual living being as a rectangle whose one side is open to Front-Appropriation (Figure 3b). We can understand the openness as an expression of sunyata.

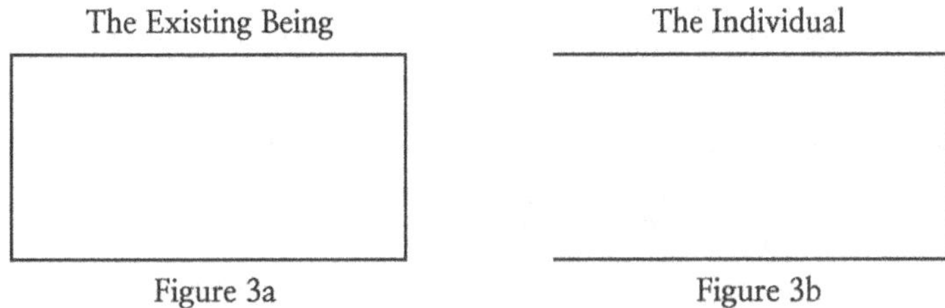

Figure 3a

Figure 3b

Since the living being cannot exist as an individual for itself alone, it is not an existing being. In order to become an existing being, however, it needs another whose Front it can appropriate unto itself. In the Figures it is clear that the individual must close its open side with a part of another individual. Its openness must be closed.

As in Figure 1 where the Front of the wall was made a constitutive part of the room, which we have called Front-Appropriation, so also in Figure 4 the individual appropriates the Front of another individual, whereby it then is shown as a closed object. In Figure 5, E-1 and E-2 are each individuals and E-2 becomes a closed rectangle, an existing being by the fact that it appropriates the front of E-1. Since, however, E-1 has not yet become an existing being, E-2, which is dependent upon a non-existing being, consequently, also cannot yet be as an existing being in reality. In order for E-1 on its side to become an existing being, its open side must be closed with the side of another individual, that is, E-1 must appropriate another individual's Front as its own constitutive part. That means the individuals can indeed be bound together (Figure 5), but if they are bound together in linear fashion, the left side of the left individual always remains open (the left side of E-1).

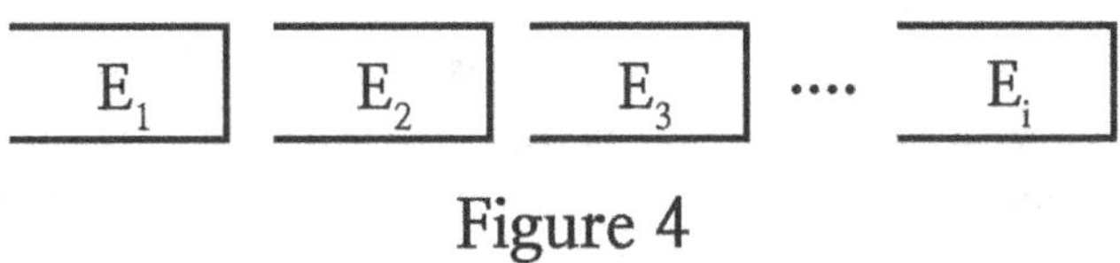

Figure 4

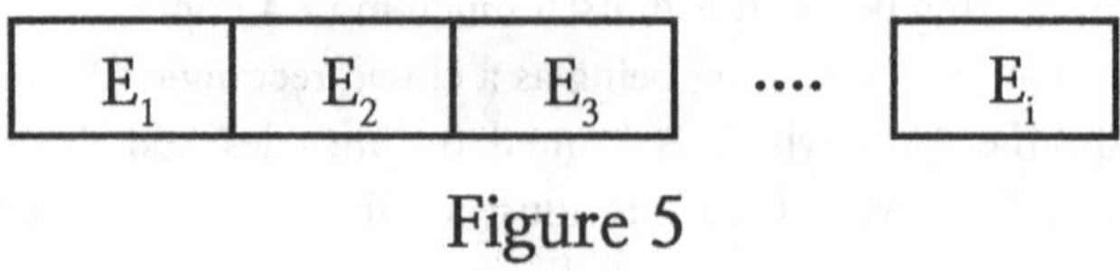

Figure 5

Then, however, the other individuals, and indeed the entirety, also cannot become existing beings (a closed rectangle). How can all become existing beings, and thus also the entirety? Obviously, they all can become existing beings only if they are not bound together in linear fashion but rather in circular fashion so that the open side of E-1 is closed by the side of the last individual (Figure 6).

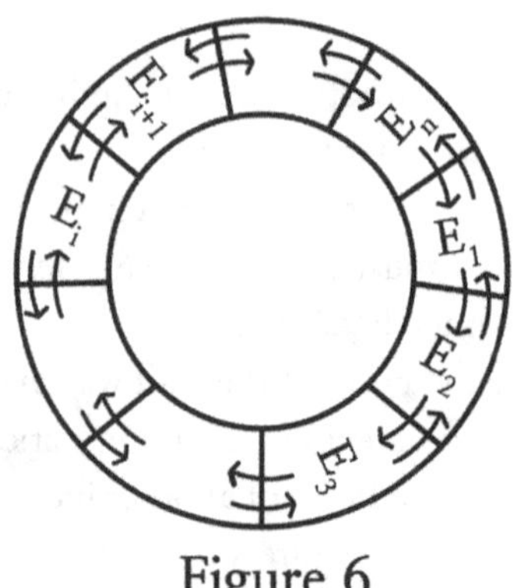

Figure 6

In Figure 6 the arrows indicate the Front-Giving and Front-Appropriation by the fact that the right front of E-n is transformed into a constitutive part of E-1, all become, through Front-Giving and Front-Appropriation, existing beings, and so likewise the entirety, which now is closed. In this Figure the relationship between the individuals are shown in an extremely simplified fashion. The circle arises not only through the fact that each individual gives its Front to the left and receives a Front from the right, but also by the fact that the Front-Giving and Front-Appropriation takes place in the reverse direction.

The Front-Structure can, however, arise between any individual and between our circle and its surroundings. Therefore, we ought to present our Figure not with a circle but rather with a large sphere. However, for the sake of simplicity we will restrict ourselves to the circle. According to it, the entirety becomes an existing being when the individuals bind themselves together in circular fashion and engage in mutual Front-Exchange. Then one sees how the Front-Giving of one individual at the same time makes possible its own existence. In other words, the causality is not linear but circular. This is fundamentally the case with every living being.

The heartbeat enables all other organs to function. They in turn provide the condition needed so that the heart can continue to beat. In our circle every individual mediately creates the possibility of its own existence in that it gives its own Front to other individuals for appropriation. This circle illustrates, therefore, the condition of co-existence of the individuals which for themselves alone are non-existing beings, but through the Front-Exchange can take on existence as existing beings.

Sunyata and *Pratītyasamutpāda*

We can learn a great deal from this circle. We will, however, limit our reflection to the dimension of sunyata. Buddhism perceives reality from the viewpoint of *pratītyasamutpāda.*[13] It was understood by Nagarjuna as "mutual dependence and relatedness," by Tendai Buddhism (Japanese; in Chinese: *T'ien-T'aitsung*) as "one *soku* many" and by Kegon Buddhism (Japanese; in Chinese: *Hua-yen-tsung*) as "the endlessly-multiple in-one-another of existing beings and effects." What those each mean we will see later. First, we want to look at how Nagarjuna's famous "negation of the four sentences" is illuminated by this circle. The "negation of the four sentences" consists of the following four negative sentences which by way of a *via negativa* speak of the entirety of *pratītyasamutpāda.*

1. The entirety of the *pratītyasamutpāda* is not "being."
2. It is not "non-being."
3. It is not "being and non-being."
4. It is not "non-being and non-non-being."

Present-day logicians often hold these "fourfold negations" often as nonsense.[14] Nevertheless, it is not mere nonsense. We will explain this by way of our circle. We interpret Nagarjuna such that he sketches a logical space which is constituted by being and non-being. For the objects "a" and "b" divide a logical space into four areas: "ab'," "ab," "a'b" and "a'b'" (Figure 7A). We can in like manner imagine for ourselves a logical space in which the concepts "being" and "non-being" are specified without asking whether that is logically or ontologically possible. Then we will have the four areas in which Nagarjuna's *Pratītyasamutpāda* has no place (Figure 7B): “sn’” (being), “s’n” (non-being), “sn” (being and non-being), “s’n’” (non-being and non-non-being).

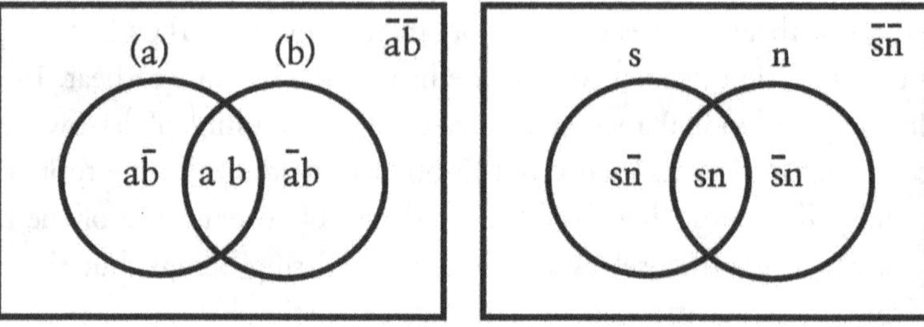

Figure 7

Since, however, these four areas fill out the entire logical space, every part which is defined with “s” and “n” must be found within it. It is therefore impossible that something which is defined with “s” and “n” would not find itself within our space. However, according to Nagarjuna, *Pratītyasamutpāda* of existing beings and non-existing beings has no place in it. Consequently, the logicians object to the fourfold negation of Nagarjuna. Nevertheless, we wish to test it by means of our circle.

1. Our circle consists of individuals, that is, from non-existing beings. When seen as a whole, it is not to be viewed as existing: The circle is not “being.”
2. However, the individual as a non-existing being nevertheless becomes an existing being because it transforms another individual’s Front into its own constituent part, since in the Front-Structure, the individual is an existing being—all the individuals are existing beings, so that the whole also is to be viewed as an existing being constituted by existing beings: The circle is not “non-being.”
3. If in our circle we hold any particular individual to be an individual, that is, a non-existing being, then we must hold all of the constitutive parts of the circle likewise to be non-existing beings. In this case the circle would consist of rectangles each of which have one open side. In that case, in this collection there would be no beings existing of themselves (closed rectangles). Thus, the circle is composed not partly of non-existing beings, and partly of existing beings. In this sense it is not “being and non-being.”

4. We can view the circle as a collection which consists of closed rectangles. Then in the circle there are no "non-existing beings." In this sense the circle is composed not partly of non-existing beings, and partly of existing beings (non-non-existing beings). Then in this sense it is likewise not "non-being and non-non-being."

Thus, we can see how the fourfold negation of Nagarjuna is validated by our circle. The secret consists of course in the ambivalence that an individual as an in itself non-existing being can at the same time through Front-Appropriation exist as an existing being.

Can we then with our circle explain the famous thesis of the *Prajñāpāramitāhrdaya Sutra*: *Yad rupam sa sunyata, ya sunyata tad rupam* (whatever is an existing being with form, that is emptiness-openness. What is emptiness-openness, that is an existing being with form)?[15] We will see in the following: *Rupa* refers to that which is there in particular form, and sunyata is, as mentioned, nullity, emptiness or non-substantiality on account of which an existing being (*rupa*) allows the penetration into itself of another, and is therefore openness as the fundamental character or fundamental nature of our reality.

Then we can interpret *sunyata* in our manner and say that sunyata means the possibility and reality of the Front-Structure in general. Then we hardly have to spell out the explanation of the thesis *Rupam sunyata, sunyata rupam.* Let me, nevertheless, try to clarify the thesis. Our "circle" is a collection of rectangles, each of which has an open side. That the individual as a rectangle is drawn as a rectangle with an open side means that it is not an existing being which exists of itself, but rather is a non-existing being. However, because the individuals mutually engage in the Front-Giving and Front-Appropriation, that is, in the Front-Structure form a circle, they can exist as existing beings, so that likewise the whole can be drawn as existing. The Front-Giving and Front-Appropriation, however, means that the individuals transform the Front of the other into their own constitutive parts so that each part, each slice of the individual, is at once the Front of another individual (see below). There is nothing in it which belongs exclusively to it. Thus, no individual—and this is also true of the circle as a whole, is a substance.

Therefore, through our circle we can see the following: that there are existing beings means that they are empty-open. Emptiness-openness, however, does not mean it exists as an objective reality alongside existing beings, but rather, that the individual (in the Front-Structure) is there in a particular form. Therefore, one can say that sunyata is nothing other than *rupa*, but also that *rupa* means nothing other than sunyata. When we posit a specific existing being in a particular form, we thereby likewise posit emptiness-openness (as the condition of its being in Front-Exchange), and when we posit emptiness-openness, we thereby posit a specific being existing there in a particular form, without which the emptiness-openness would be a mere nothing.

Chinese Buddhism developed further the conceptualization of Nagarjuna, namely, the conceptualization of sunyata as non-substantiality. Tendai Buddhism (Chinese: *T'ien-T'ai-tsung*),[16] as mentioned, expressed the thesis: "one *soku* many." That was a central expression of its understanding of *Pratītyasamutpāda*: "The one is there as the many," or: "The whole of reality can from one viewpoint be understood as the one, but also from another viewpoint as the many." The structure of the whole of reality is understood to be like our body, which consists of many members, but which at the same time is one body (cf. 1 Cor 12). From our circle we can easily see that. For our circle as a whole is one object, which, however, is composed of many individuals, whereby the whole and the individuals are dependent upon one another. The rather complicated system of the T'ien-Tai philosophy can here be left aside.

Kegon Buddhism (Chinese: *Hua-yen-tsung*)[17] discusses the mutual relationship of existing beings in greater detail. It presents the following thesis as its understanding of *Pratītyasamutpāda* above all: "The endlessly multiple in-one-another of existing beings and their effects." The world of *Pratītyasamutpāda* is compared to infinitely many mirrors which reflect one another infinitely. We can also see this from our circle. If in it we take as an example the Front-Giving and Front-Appropriation from left to right, the giving and taking move from left to right in the circle, and indeed endlessly so. One can also say the same thing of the movement from right to left: One can take a slice from any individual, for example, in E-1. Then there gather here the Front of all individuals, not only the Front of the individual on the right or on the left side, but rather the Fronts of all the individuals, for through the Front-Appropriation the Front of, for example, E-1 is transferred and expanded through E-2 and the following E3-n until E-1, and indeed endlessly. Our circle, of course, is a model. However, we see the same relationship in the circular causality of our body. Thus, one can say that the understanding of the *Pratītyasamutpāda* in Kegon Buddhism can be expressed with our model. It is interesting to observe here that in such endless being in one another the whole is reproduced in small fashion in each individual insofar as in each individual the Fronts of all individuals are present (one should recall that the Fronts of innumerable stars gather together at each point on the earth, or that the Fronts of all the organs of a body gather together at each point of the body). The one can correspond to the whole. In similar manner the Leibnizian monad reflects the whole. However, it has no "window,"[18] so that it presents the whole as such only from itself, while in our model all the individuals are open to a real in-one-another. We must further call attention to the fact that, in Kegon Buddhism, *Pratītyasamutpāda* is conceived as event, as happening, and that happening is borne by the "life of Buddha." Its interpretation of the whole of reality is thus analogous to the Pauline interpretation of the church as the body of Christ: The Christian church is a happening in the world that is borne by the life of Christ. (We will let the complicated worldview of Kegon Buddhism as a whole aside here.)

What is *Zen*? The praxis of Zen-sitting, *Jhana*, is something pre-Buddhist. Early Buddhism, probably already Gautama Buddha himself, had taken it up and made it into a central praxis. Nevertheless, Zen Buddhism first arose in China. Its beginnings lie in darkness. Historically it can be confirmed that Zen established itself in China as an independent Buddhism through Eno (Japanese; in Chinese: Hui-neng, 638–713 CE), the sixth patriarch of Zen Buddhism, and reached its highpoint in the Tang period (618–906). Chinese Zen produced two streams. From one stream, which began with Nangaku Ejo (Japanese; in Chinese: Nanyueh Huai-Jang, a disciple of Eno) and his disciple Baso Doitsu (709–788), there came Rinzai (Japanese; in Chinese: Lin-chi, ?–866). His Zen was brought by the Japanese Eisai (1141–1215) as "Rinzai Zen" to Japan. From this stream through Hakuin (1685–1768) until today important masters have come forth. From the other stream, which began with Seigen Gyoshi (?–740), another disciple of Eno and his disciple Sekito Kisen (700–790), came Dogen (1200–1253), the founder of Japanese Soto-Zen, which likewise has developed into a large community.[19]

Zen rejects neither the philosophy of Tendai Buddhism ("one *soku* many"), nor that of Kegon Buddhism ("the endlessly in-one-another of existing beings and their effects"). The latter in fact has a central position in Zen. What, however, makes Zen Buddhism to be Zen Buddhism is not a new theory, but rather the enlightenment, that is, the "awakening" to the "life of the Buddha," namely, to the life which bears the whole in the Front-Structure. The characteristic of Zen lies in the *immediacy* of its awareness of, to put it in our language, "Front-Structure," and therefore of the "life of Buddha," so to say, in one's own body. Here is the great turning from objectifying knowledge to awakening—self-awakening. Zen, therefore, means to understand oneself in the in-one-another of subject and object, in the circle of the Front-Exchange, and to be awake to what the whole dynamic circle bears—to the life of Buddha in human beings so the Front-Structure is not grasped merely intellectually, but rather as the reality of one's life with one's entire body.

Before we go further let us observe several important characteristics or specifications of Mahayana Buddhism as they have been worked out by several scholars to see whether or not they also are true of our circle. If they hold true of them, we can say that our circle represents Buddhist matter.

First of all, Daisetsu Suzuki (1870–1966), using the Diamond *Prajñāpāramitā* Sutra, formulated the thinking pattern of the early Mahayana Buddhism in the following formula: "A is not A, therefore it is called A."[20] In order to clarify the sentence let us take any individual in our circle, for example, E-1. Then in this individual, as we have seen above, the Fronts of not only E-n and E-2, but the Fronts of all individuals are gathered together, and indeed endlessly so. What then should E-1 be called? It is not simply E-1, since the Fronts of all other individuals represent these in it, and indeed in such a way that in these Fronts we encounter the other individuals. Therefore, A is not purely self-identical A, namely, not something which is A and nothing other than A. Nevertheless, as such an individual in which the Fronts of all other individuals are found A is A, just as the Fronts of all other organs are found in the heart, and precisely as such the heart is the heart. It is clear, therefore, that the formula of D. Suzuki is true of our circle.

According to Tokuryu Yamanouchi[21] the characteristic of Mahayana Buddhist thinking lies in its *via negativa* manner of expression, above all in the phrase "neither A nor non-A." We have seen a typical example from Nagarjuna with his "neither being nor non-being." According to Yamanouchi, the annulment of the principle of identity was accomplished by the synthetic judgment of Kant, and the annulment of the principle of contradiction by the dialectic of Hegel. However, the annulment of the principle of the excluded middle has not taken place in the tradition of European philosophy. Nevertheless, we can point to the fact that this phrase, "neither A nor non-A," can often be found among the mystics, for example, Nicholas Cusanus.[22] Also, according to Paul, a Christian is neither simply a human being nor Christ, in the sense that he is he, because it is no longer he but Christ who lives in him (Gal 2:20f.). However, it has been shown that the individual in our circle is neither an existing being nor a non-existing being. Later on, when we discuss the relationship between Transcendence and the individual in Mahayana Buddhism it will be further shown that an individual is neither merely "this worldly" nor merely "other worldly." From our in-one-another of an existing being, through which non-A is allowed to arise precisely as the indispensable moment of A, it can be affirmed: "Neither A nor non-A."

Koshiro Tamaki (born 1915) showed that it was not first in Mahayana Buddhism that enlightenment was seen as the essence of Buddhism, but already was held to be so by Gautama Buddha.[23] Truth radiates not only the reason and heart, but the entire person, with its corporeality, is radiated by dharma, the "truth," in that the pure self-identity of being-a-person is denied, and the being-a-person in relationship to all other existing beings is revealed. It then also becomes clear that the entire being-a-person is borne by Transcendence.

We hardly need to spend any time explaining this statement. It is important for us, however, to ascertain that the enlightenment, or awakening, is not a matter merely of the reason or self-clarification of the reason, but rather that it deals with the entire person in its corporeality, that the body, so to speak, understands itself. That is, the human being knows itself to be borne in its entire bodily reality by Transcendence (Phil 1:21).[24] We have indeed determined that the Front-Structure of our existence is found in our dimension as material beings, of our existence as living beings, as persons. It is the awakening to the entirety of our being human that Zen above all aims at radically achieving.

We have thus shown how our concept of Front-Structure corresponds to *Pratītyasamutpāda*.

We will now look briefly at the *destruction of the Front-Structure.* There naturally are many possibilities for this, but we will here indicate only typical forms.

Take, for example, that an individual wishes to take, that is, appropriate to itself another's Front, but not give, not turn over its Front to another for appropriation. What happens then? This individual cannot exist alone. Therefore, the following structure must result (Figure 8).

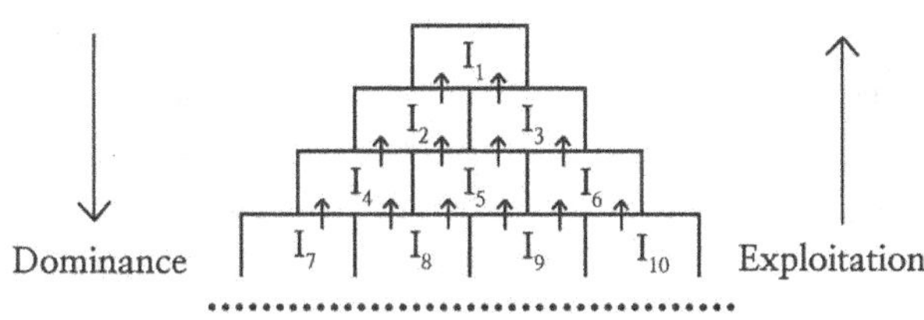

Figure 8

I-1 lives by exploiting I-2 and I-3: I-1 needs many individuals in order to live from their exploitation. I-2 and I-3 on their side, although the Front-Structure may exist between them, exploit other individuals in that they dominate these human beings.

This is obviously the structure of exploitation and one-sided dominance. This structure can arise not merely between individuals, but also between classes, states and also between human beings and nature. The mere Ego, which fundamentally wishes only to take but not to give, wishes to dominate in this manner. In fact, this structure existed, for example, between free persons and slaves in the Roman Empire, between the feudal lords and their serfs in the Middle Ages, between the capitalists and the workers according to Karl Marx, between the sexes and between the industrialized human being and nature today. In this structure the lower individuals must work more than would be necessary, for they are one-sidedly exploited. Further, if several pyramids exist next to each other, one will want to dominate over the other so that they must struggle among themselves. This structure thus brings forth constant wars, and thereby suffering and misfortune. The foundation of suffering and misfortune lies not in this structure alone. However, history manifoldly shows what evil this structure has caused. This structure runs contrary to the fundamental orientation of the human beings, who exist in constant Front-Exchange with one another. In the end, however, this structure is destined for collapse, since the exploited ones below will be so emptied out that finally they will no longer be able to bear those above.

There are at least two other important forms of destruction:

1. The individuals separate from one another so that the circle is dissolved. They become isolated. Since, however, as isolated beings they cannot live, they form a society on the basis of their specific interests, which again leads to the pyramid structure. Otherwise they will remain isolated.
2. The individuals do not wish to dominate, but rather to depend upon the rich or strong. That is another form in which the individuals wish to take more than to give. Instead of dominating and they themselves exploiting, they flatter. That happens also when the dominating ones of one pyramid encounter a stronger pyramid. Isolation and dependency destroy the circle of the normal of the Front-Exchange. The destruction of the Front-Structure on its side confirms that this fundamental structure of life is indispensable to life. In fact, the Front-Exchange occurs in the natural activity of living. The animals and plants carry it out themselves. The human being, however, must be wakened to the fundamental orien-

tation of life. In this context it is important to point out that each one in our circle must have his or her individuality. They must have their own capabilities, their own character, which distinguishes them from others. That lies at the very basis of the circle. Among those that are identical there can be no Front-Exchange. Since the heart and the lungs function differently, a Front-Exchange between them can take place. Therefore, the individuals in our circle must have their own individuality so that they can completely develop their own possibilities, and in such a way that this individuality specifically enables the Front-Exchange and does not destroy it, or in such a way that they can take their own place in the circle where they can carry out the Front-Exchange. For it is not so that they can carry it out in any arbitrarily chosen place. It is like a note, which has its own place in a piece of music and would disturb the entire piece if it were in a false position. Our circle then is no totalitarian system in which freedom and individuality are suppressed. It is, however, also not a society of "anything goes," in which ordered living together is not attended to. Love and freedom go hand in hand in our circle.

The Ego and Its Differentiating Intellect

The Front-Structure is usually hidden from us. That comes about because our daily language gives only the identical side of the Front-Structure expression and leaves aside the other, contradictory side. We have become acquainted with the Buddhist *Soku*. *Soku* means "is/ is-not." This *Soku* comes into existence in the Front-Structure. The appropriation by A of non-A's Front validates "A *Soku* non-A" (A is/is not A), while in our everyday language "A is A" and "A is not non-A." In our circle (Figure 6) we have further seen that the individual is not a self-identical object since there is present in it the Fronts of other individuals, in which the first individual encounters others. We have further seen that every component in our circle is neither an existing being nor a non-existing being, that insofar as it is an individual it must not be viewed as an existing being, while it is at the same time nevertheless an existing being insofar as it can be presented as a closed figure. Thus, we can say that the proposition which expresses the Front-Structure is in its form contrary to the three principles of traditional logic—here we repeat, however, immediately that we do not completely eliminate the principle of contradiction. For we see that from one point of view A is A, but from another point of view it is at the same time non-A. In this, however, we must note that these two points of view stand in a relationship of *Soku* to one another: Both are indeed to be distinguished from one another, but not to be separated—as the two poles of a magnet or the two sides of a piece of paper.

The three principles of traditional logic are important in our connection for they exhibit the essence of our daily language. They are as follows: the principle of identity (A is A), the principle of contradiction (A is not non-A), and the principle of the excluded middle (there is nothing which is neither A nor non-A). We can take these principles as the guarantee of unequivocalness. In order to be unequivocal A must positively be A. It can be, however, that A is, at the same time, non-A. Then the unequivocalness of A is lost. Therefore, A may not be, at the same time, non-A. If, however, A is really A and non-A, there nevertheless can be a third (the "middle") which is neither A nor non-A. Then A can be this third, so that the unequivocalness of A again is lost. Therefore, there may not be this third ("middle") if A is unequivocally to be A. Therefore, if A is unequivocally to be A, the demands of all three principles must be fulfilled. These principles in the end show how concepts and prepositions must be formed in order to be clear and distinct. They, however, are not automatically ontologically intended. If they had full ontological validity, then the Eleatics would have been correct: there can be no movement, no change. However, only to the extent that we read these principles ontologically into reality—either consciously or unconsciously—do we lose the Front-Structure from our view.

We can here ask what reality would look like if it could be adequately described with the language, which in any respect, takes the form of the demands of traditional logic. We respond: If, for example, reality consisted of classical atoms, which were simple, unchanged and also purely self-identical substances, then it clearly could be adequately represented with univocal language. Or we could say: If complex reality were so structured that it could be reduced to simple, unchanged, self-identical and substantial elements or objects, the concepts and principles would also be unequivocal in form.

Since, however, life has Front-Structure, the language which speaks of it must break with the demands of unequivocalness, although we strive to preserve unequivocalness from a particular point of view.

We observe here further the following: The three principles of traditional logic provide the conditions under which things can be classified. If A is A and not non-A, if further there is no third which is neither A nor non-A, then a thing belongs either to A or to non-A. Thus, things can be unequivocally classified whereas in the Front-Structure, non-A's Front appropriated by A obviously belongs to A and non-A. We call, then, the intellect which solely uses unequivocal language with the conscious or unconscious presupposition that it is an adequate instrument for the description of our reality in every regard, the "differentiating intellect."[25]

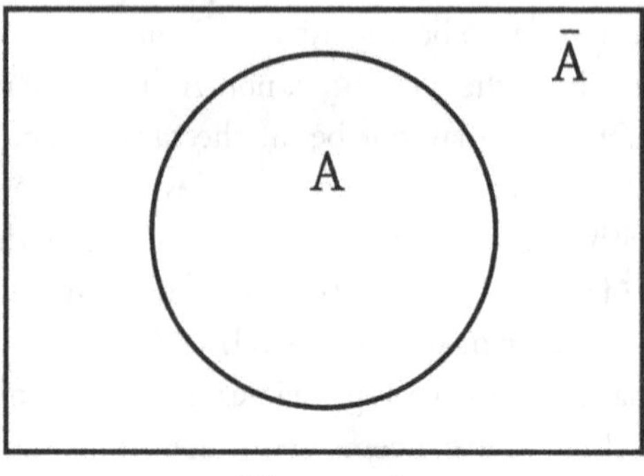

Figure 9

We do not dispute that the differentiating intellect with its unequivocal language is indispensable for our life. We make use of the unequivocal language in gaining information. It is understandable that information must be unequivocal, otherwise it could not function as information. Likewise, agreements must be unequivocal. Every agreement and every consensus, such as ethics and laws, must be unequivocal or as unequivocal as possible. The language of the law must be free of contradiction. Otherwise the system of law destroys itself. What does this say? This means that unequivocal language is indispensable in our social life since it is constantly in need of information and consensus. The same is also true for our behavior in general: We do not know *a priori* how we should behave in a given situation. What I have to do in a situation I have learned *a posteriori*, because we do not live instinctively. Instinct has been almost entirely destroyed for the human being. Therefore, what is to be done needs to be unequivocally specified by principles. The human being takes a position in social life which has a specific role attached to it. In this the role given him must be as unequivocal as possible. How a human being in a society should behave toward a specific person must likewise be unequivocally specified so that the society can function in an orderly manner. In other words, in our living together, identity is the essence of a person. The personal name is already a sign of this. What someone is, what someone has, what someone must do, all that must be unequivocally clear. Otherwise we do not know how we should behave toward a specific person in a given situation. The destruction of this unequivocalness would be a threat to the order of a society or to living together in general: What belongs to one human being belongs to her or him and not to another. How a man behaves toward his wife must be different than his behavior toward other women, etc.

The unequivocalness of language is, moreover, demanded because it is indispensable for the human beings who live, speak, and work together. By work here I include work involving technology. Technology applies knowledge, and specifically causal knowledge. It converts causality into teleology. Technology utilizes a knowledge in which whenever the condition "p" exists, then "q" always happens. This knowledge again must be unequivocal and irreversible, otherwise it would not be usable. Here we should recall that the fourth principle of traditional logic is the principle of sufficient reason and is the foundation of causal thinking. Then all four principles of traditional logic give expression to the locus of the unequivocalness of our language and our thinking: In the cohabitation of speaking and working human beings. It is thereby the postulate of our living together. This has to do with the fact that causality and the idea of pure objectivity are constructions of our thinking, and that they have been projected into the reality in which we working human beings live together. The human being also projects substantiality into reality, or reads it out of the rich complexity of reality because it is postulated in our unequivocal language. Then the "individual" without any hesitation is taken to mean the "existing being." For we are unconsciously oriented by unequivocal language, are always inclined to think and to say that A, independent from non-A, is completely of itself A, which doubtless is a misuse of unequivocal language.

We can establish that the apes had developed themselves to the species of *Homo sapiens* when they began to speak and produce working instruments in an ordered living together. With this, unequivocal language has its roots in being human itself. However, in the measure in which unequivocal language, and thereby the differentiating intellect, dominate, the Front-Structure as the fundamental structure of life is left out of view. Then the original life is replaced by the activity of the differentiating intellect. Thus, for example, love as a will to life through which the fundamental structure of life is grounded, is replaced by customs, morals, and laws. To that extent the differentiating intellect with its unequivocal language becomes the ultimate subject of the human being. In the time of Jesus, for example, certain streams within Judaism were inclined to control the entirety of human living by law in such a way that the law replaced the will of God. Jesus perceived herein the basis of the inauthenticity of the human being.

The intellect is a property of the Ego. What is the Ego? The Ego is the subject of the human being insofar as one is conscious in oneself that one is doing what one is doing. I am conscious that I now am writing this book. Therefore, I as Ego am acting. When I dream I am not aware of that fact, but rather find myself in the world of the dream. Hence, I am not the one who produces the dream. The dream comes out of the unconscious, not out of my Ego. In contrast, I am aware of the fact that I am acting or that I am in control when I perceive something, speak, think, and decide. What does that mean? The Ego is placed between the outer and inner world. In instinctive life a reaction is a priori connected with the stimulus. That is, naturally, not the case with human beings. In principle, the reaction within the human being is separate from the stimulus. The Ego acts to understand the situation, to reflect, and to decide. In the human being instinct is replaced by the Ego. That the Ego is conscious of what it does means that feedback is of the essence of the Ego insofar as it reacts to the situation and, in examining the effects of the reaction, controls its action. Thus, the intellect and its thinking belong to the Ego; they are its property. The question arises, however: How does the Ego understand itself when it conceives itself with the differentiating intellect and its language which is unequivocal in every respect? It is clear that it understands itself as self-identical, namely, as that which is nothing other than Ego. "I am I," is the fundamental statement of the Ego. The Ego is always inclined to understand itself as that which is based on itself: a substance which is separate from other individuals. It reads unequivocalness, substantiality and self-identity into the individuals which it encounters. Thus arises "the world" in which it works with the differentiating intellect. The unequivocal language and the Ego condition each other. We will call the Ego which has arisen in this manner "the mere Ego," that Ego which is based on itself because it separates itself from, or leaves out of consideration, that which takes place in the human being's Front-Structure. It is there, isolated. It is concerned now only with itself, it cares only for itself.

The mere Ego is the Ego in the sense of egoism. We could outline here a phenomenology of egoism, however, we will limit ourselves to the most essential: The mere Ego is self-conscious and based on itself. However, it has no real foundation for its existence since the individual can be an existing being only in the Front-Structure. The mere Ego wishes to know nothing of this. The Ego is not free of anxiety. It draws for itself an ideal picture which it attempts to make real. Now being can be divided into three elements: *existentia*, *essentia*, and *potentia*. Therefore, the mere Ego wants to hold on to and strengthen itself in these. It wishes to secure its *existentia* through possessions and riches. It wishes to secure its *essentia* through fame. It wishes to realize its *potentia* through power. Thus, it seeks for riches, fame, and power. Further, since the Ego is the subject of feelings, the mere Ego wishes to enjoy life. To its enjoyment belongs first of all self-enjoyment. Since the Ego is self-conscious it wishes to observe itself and, like Narcissus, enjoy itself in self-admiration. It belongs to the very nature of the mere Ego that it is proud of itself, being ignorant of itself and others. It wishes not only to make itself secure, dispose of reality, and enjoy it, but it wishes to become a conqueror. Not only the strong but also the weak wish to conquer.[26] Here its illusion arises or is confirmed. For the Ego which is built only upon itself is—like the world formed by the differentiating intellect—in itself an illusion. Nevertheless, the mere Ego must justify itself. It needs self-justification for its self-description and its self-realization. It does so in illusionary fashion: It interprets everything so it can create a justification for its existence. In this manner it distorts reality. It wishes to. And yet, it likewise hides this distortion from itself. It does not wish to know anything of that. In this Nietzsche was completely right in his insight that the will to power maintains itself through the fact that it justifies, supports, strengthens itself through its interpretation of reality, that, in fact, the view of the world in general arises from this interpretation and that there is no truth at all in it. This is true of the self-description and explanations of being by Egoism. However, how far can a human being be liberated from Egoism?

Transcendence and the Human Being

The Vow of Life

In egoism, the direct self-affirmation of the Ego and the differentiating intellect are bound together. Together with the differentiating intellect, the Ego understands itself as the mere Ego, while the mere Ego, in order to be able to affirm itself, outlines a world over which it has control through the differentiating intellect. The self-affirmation of the mere Ego, however, dissolves, indeed, dies in the faith in the savior, and the faith also leads to the overcoming of the differentiating intellect. The overcoming of the mere Ego, however, on its side occurs in the enlightenment (the awakening) and this brings with it the dissolution of the self-affirmation of the mere Ego so that in both cases the bond between egoism and the differentiating intellect is broken off.

The consequence of faith in both Christianity and Jodo-Buddhism[27] is the Ego giving up self-affirmation through and of itself, but not in such a way that the one performing the self-giving is not oneself given, thereby remaining outside of the gift, but, rather, such that the one giving becomes aware that the Ego is not a final subject, and the entire human being is affirmed, borne by Transcendence. That is the meaning of Tariki (the powerful action of the other, that is, of Amida) in Jodo-Buddhism. "It is no longer I who live, but Christ who lives in me; and the life I now live in the flesh I live by faith in the Son of God, who loved me and gave himself for me" (Gal 2:20) is another expression of this. With this, self-existence's unequivocalness is lifted: That I exist means that I have died and Christ (in the case of Jodo-Buddhism, Amida) lives in me.[28] Now the sole domination of the Ego and the differentiating intellect with its completely unequivocal language is at an end.

Enlightenment means to understand oneself to be in the circle of existing beings, to comprehend oneself in the Front-Structure so that a person is understood as one pole whose counter-pole is always the "object," the "thou" who one constantly encounters. Understanding oneself as a pole means that one recognizes one cannot exist without the counter-pole whose Front is found within. That leads to the dissolution of the mere Ego's direct self-assertion as if it were an *atomon* (*individuum*) in the classical sense. With this, the sole domination of a mere Ego is at an end.

The dissolution of the mere Ego and the overcoming of the sole domination of the differentiating intellect leads then to the recognition that the Self is borne by Transcendence. This, however, means, in the third place—strange as it may sound—the reconciliation of the Ego with its own body and its own corporeality. The body is not always oriented in a friendly fashion toward the mere Ego, or even for the "enjoying" Ego along with the differentiating intellect. Often it offers resistance. When the Ego attempts through its will to make use of the body and dominate it, the body resists. In the measure in which the Ego, with its abstract will, wishes to dominate itself, it degrades its body to mere flesh which then puts up all the more resistance. Therefore, overcoming of the mere Ego—which takes place in both faith and enlightenment—leads to reconciliation with the body. The human person understands themself then no longer as an abstract spirit (reason, will), but rather as life.

In fact, "life" is a fundamental word in both the New Testament and in Jodo-Buddhism. For Paul, the body is the dwelling place of the Holy Spirit (see 1 Cor 3:6). In Buddhism, salvation—authenticity—of the human being is never understood in the separation (liberation) of the thinking psyche from the body, other than, for example, in the Hellenistic religions. For Buddhism, the view that the Ego is as a thinking substance immortal in itself is an insanity. If, however, the Ego has become reconciled with the body, how does it then understand itself? Life manifests itself in it as that which "wills" to form a circle of existing beings. Moreover, it does so in such a way that the individual—in order for the individual's possibilities, that is, their individuality, to develop—is at once a pole in the circle, while the circle for its part integrates every individual into itself.

We wish to call this "will" of life which is based on its fundamental orientation, the "vow of Life." "Vow" is of course a fundamental word of Jodo-Buddhism, according to which the Amida-Buddha took the vow to found the "Pure Land" to which every confessing believer who called on the name of the Amida-Buddha will go after his or her death and will attain enlightenment through Amida-Buddha. In Jodo-Buddhism the vow of the Amida is something powerful which will certainly realize itself in such a way that humans can trust in this realization. The concept "vow" is closely related in meaning to the Hebrew Bible concept of Emeth[29] as "that which realizes itself on the basis of the will of God." Thus, we prefer the concept of "vow" to the concept of "will." Moreover, several Zen Buddhists who are sympathetic toward Jodo-Buddhism see in the activities of Life, as for example the blooming of a flower, the vow of the Amida at work.[30] The vow of Life is the concern of life, not the concern of the mere reason.

The Ego is the place where the vow of Life manifests itself and is revealed. When the vow of Life manifests itself in it, the vow of Life becomes the vow of the particular human being concerned. The vow of Life is hidden from the mere Ego which has distanced and alienated itself from life since the mere Ego is fixed only upon itself. However, it is of the essence of Life that it enlightens itself. Self-consciousness arises from this, but it is really first self-understanding and enlightenment that do. Human life is that life which is conscious of itself, which understands itself—therefore, that life in which Life brings its essence to light. Life and light belong together. Christ, but also the Amida-Buddha, are both eternal Life and light, the ground of the self-enlightening Life of the individual human person. It is only together with the light that Life is authentic Life. Light without Life is an abstraction, and Life without light is demonic since life then becomes a dark drive. Life and light cannot dispense with each other. Here we see how philosophy and religion postulate each other.

Further, it is clear why enlightenment, awakening, is absolutely necessary. Transcendence works upon the human being in every moment. However, insofar as the human being is not aware of that, no conscious "willing" in the sense of the vow of Life can be affected in him or her. God had indeed "chosen Paul from his mother's womb and called him through his grace," but before God revealed his son to Paul, Paul persecuted the primitive church (see Gal 1:13–16). As, however, the Son of God was revealed in him and over against him, Paul became the proclaimer of the Gospel. He recognized that his mission was ultimately affected by Christ so that he could say Christ carried the mission "through [him]" (Rom 15:18). Only when the human being awakens to the vow of Life[31] affected by Transcendence will it become his or her own vow. Self-understanding, self-awakening is the conditio sine qua non of authentic Life. For, in fact, understanding belongs to human life. Culture arises only insofar as it is understood. That is, for example, the case with music: For those who do not understand it, music remains a mere string of sounds. The sense of a text does not exist if one cannot read it. That is also true of a human person's heart, which can have an effect on another person only when it is understood. Not to understand a human being is to leave them in the lurch. This is because the human being can only then rightly live when rightly understanding life.

If human beings awaken to the vow of Life, they find joy in the Front-Exchange. They wish to understand themselves in common existence with other existing beings. The vow of Life now becomes their own vow: Now they desire it themselves. The "thou shalt" of the law can be replaced by "I want to," or "I take the vow," for the law is really the expression of the vow of Life. This being awakened can, as noted,[32] be deepened to an awareness that the life of each individual human being is borne by Transcendence. Let me cite again the Christian parallel to this in the words of Paul: "It is no longer I who live, but Christ who lives in me" (Gal 2:20). "For me to live is Christ" (Phi 1:21). Paul recognized that all of his life activities were borne by Christ. One is also reminded in this how Rinzai (Linchi) spoke of the inner activity of the formless: The Formless in the body confirmed itself in the eye as seeing, in the ear as hearing, in the mouth as speaking, in the hands as grasping, and in the feet as walking. Rinzai had become aware that in all a human being's life activities, the Formless is present.[33]

The vow of Life which lies at the basis of our life activity aims at forming and completing the circle of the living. It transcends the individuals. This vow of Life is the work of Transcendence. For it is God who in each of you affects both the willing and the working in order to accomplish his own good will (cf. Phi 2:13). The vow of Life, which is revealed in individual human beings as their own vow, is not a heteronomous power. Moreover, it is also not something of the mere reason, not to speak of the mere self-will. The human being which takes the vow understands itself to be so formed that the vow of Life realizes itself through the individual human being, but also as the individual human being.

The Front of Transcendence and the Self

The Relationship Between Transcendence and the Human Being

The recognition of the vow of Life being borne by Transcendence is common to both Buddhism and Christianity. In my view, however, Christianity has analyzed the vow of Life in a sense more precisely than has Buddhism. The dogmas of the Trinity and Christology find here their proper place. Thus, we wish in this section to briefly undertake this analysis so as to move from Buddhist thinking to Christian. We will in the process of the Front-Exchange become aware that this process itself is borne by Transcendence. We have a Christian expression for this in the New Testament: "For love is of God, and he who loves is born of God and knows God" (1 John 4:7). The vow of Life to form the circle of the living manifests itself in human beings as love, as the original, immediate affirmation of one's fellow human beings and the joyful will to a convivial existence. Knowledge (self-understanding) grounds itself immediately in the revelation of the vow of Life. In brief: In the Front-Exchange's original life activities, human beings become aware of the vow of Life and see Transcendence at work there.[34] Then they understand themselves from that perspective and become aware of how Transcendence effects knowledge and love in human beings.

How is the relationship between Transcendence and the human being to be understood?

The one loving knows God. It is not simply that the human being is the object of God's love, but rather much more that the human being is the one loving and that, when they love, they know God, for love comes from God. The one loving knows that love is effected by God, indeed, that ultimately God loves through them, for "God is love."

God is not an existing being alongside the human being. The human being knows God when the human being loves. However, the encounter with God also means that we perceive the call of God in the words of the proclamation. On the one hand it is God who loves through me. On the other hand, it is God whom I encounter in the word of the proclamation. God is therefore on the one hand, my deepest subject. On the other, God is at the same time the one over-against me who addresses me through human beings.

Transcendence is so to speak the field of force within which the individual living being is brought to form the circle in the Front-Structure. That is, the human being is within the field of force of Transcendence. In other words, human beings are so formed that they consciously realize the vow of Life to which they awaken so that the circle comes into existence. The vow lies at the basis of the activities of Life and the human being understands this as affected by Transcendence. Now insofar as the vow becomes the vow of each individual human person, one will also become aware of the action of God in their willing and knowing. Transcendence is the ultimate subject in the human being. On the other hand, one perceives the address of God in their fellow human beings' expression of the vow of Life, which calls forth a resonance within. Transcendence is likewise the one who is over-against. Thus, Transcendence is first, the field of force in which the human being finds themself, second, the one effecting, the ultimate subject of the human being, and third, the one who addresses them through the word or deed of fellow human beings.

The relationship between the vow of Life and the Ego needs to be noted here. God gives rise in me, in my body, to the act of willing. That is, to my will. However, that does not yet imply that I must carry it out. I can ignore it, I can be disobedient. It is the Ego that decides. The Ego is never excluded from this function.

Between willing and carrying out, between the vow of Life which has manifested in one and the Ego, there is both continuity and discontinuity. Expressed otherwise, the Ego is responsible for the execution. The subjectivity of the human being has, so to say, a double structure. Transcendence is its ultimate subject, but the Ego is responsible for the expression of the vow of Life.

We must now inquire into the *structure of the "field of force."* Transcendence is the one effecting, the subject. To effect means to effect the vow of Life in human beings (the content of the effecting) and to let it work into the human being (the act of effecting). Obviously, this is a triad: "The subject of the effecting," "content of the effecting" and "the act of effecting," and each one implies the other two in itself. That is, the field of force has a triune structure.[35]

As we shall see in the next chapter, the circle is, speaking in a Christian manner, the *Communio sanctorum* as the body of Christ (cf. 1 Cor 12) in which Christ is present as its "Life." If Christ is the image of God (*Eikon theou*, see 2 Cor 4:4; Col 1:15) whose realization in historical reality is the church as the body of Christ, then it belongs to the vow of Life to form the *Communio sanctorum* as Christ as the "content of the effecting" of Transcendence. The content of the divine effecting is the structural principle of our circle.[36] If that is so, the vow of Life as a structural principle of our circle corresponds to the Logos, to the Son of God. More precisely said, the structural principle is something transcendent (*Logos*), while the vow of Life, which is transcendent-immanent (divine-human), is to be understood as the incarnate *Logos*. Here we see the distinction between the *Logos* and the incarnate as the divine-human (Christ).[37]

When the human being understands the vow of Life, which has become his or her own vow, as being effected by Transcendence, when further, the human being in his or her inner effecting is moved to the shaping of the *Communio sanctorum*, of the body of Christ, of the Lord who calls us to the forming of the church and commissions us thereto, then the "Lord" is the one whom Paul called Christ, and his "Christ in me" is now the Front of Transcendence which has been appropriated by the human being in historical reality or in the Christian (Figure 10).

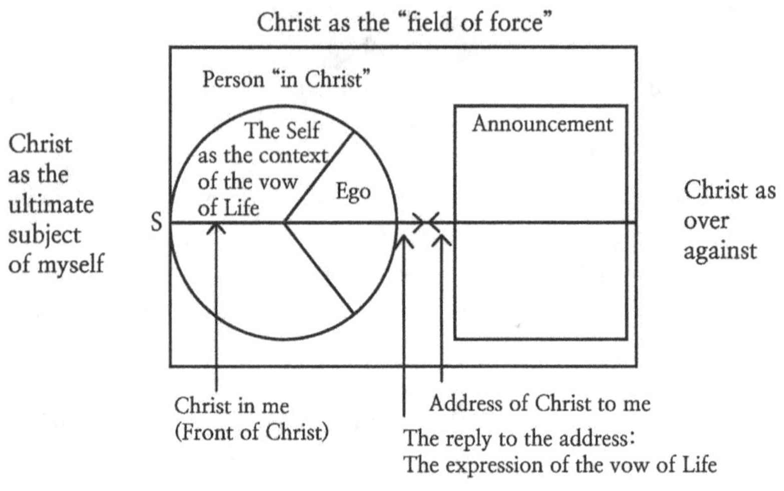

Figure 10

Above, we learned to know two types of Front-Structure: the substantial type and the wave type. Here we have the third type of Front-Structure: The Front of Transcendence constitutes the Self of the Christian. In this case the Front is neither a substance nor a wave. The *field* in which the human finds her or himself is the "field of force" (cf. "in Christ," 2 Cor 5:17) but it is also the "field of force," "effect," which is in the human being and constitutes the "Self" (cf. "Christ in," Gal 2:20). The field of *force* within the human being, however, is not merely a part of the field of *force*, but represents, rather, the entire field, generally speaking, insofar as we encounter the other itself in the Front of the other.

This in-one-another of the field and of the human being can be compared to the following: Music is no mere sum of physical tones. The tones are music in the human being's heart, and the human heart is present in music (in-one-another). The human heart is neither a substance nor a wave. However, the sound tones are integrated into music in the human heart's field of force. In the sense that the human heart makes the physical vibrations of the ear into musical tones, the human heart constitutes the musical tones, the music. In the music we perceive the human heart, the expression of which is in the music. The music is the human-physical, the human heart which has "become sound." In this regard it is an analogy of the "incarnation," or "divine-human."

Since the human heart is invisible, that is, not objectively perceivable, while a physical tone is objectively perceivable as such, we cannot place both on the same level and say that the human heart makes up one part of the music; it is not so. Nevertheless, we know that the human heart constitutes the music. That means that here the Front-Structure is between two elements of different dimensions: The music "is/is-not" the human heart. The music is the human heart insofar as the music gives expression to the human heart, and indeed in such a way that a particular dimension of the human heart is given expression precisely by the piece of music in question, and it is done thusly and in no other way, so that the human heart manifests itself as the piece of music. In this exclusive "manifesting itself as" we see the unity between the music and the human heart. This, however, is not the substantial unity of both objects. The human heart which is present in a piece of music is, more precisely spoken, human heart's Front which is one with the piece of music in the sense that the heart manifests itself as the piece of music, so that we encounter the composer's heart in the piece of music. We call this third type of Front-Structure the "field type" since the existing beings in the field of force express its act of effecting (manifest themselves as) in that the act of effecting constitutes the being-thus of the existing beings, and thereby is one with it. The act of effecting manifests itself in the being-thus of the existing beings, and in the exclusive "manifesting itself as" we see the unity of the effecting and the effected, like the unity which exists between God and Jesus in that God is manifested as Jesus.

In this manner we can also grasp the unity between "the Transcendence in me" and the human being. Transcendence and the human being are one in that this unity manifests itself as the "circle" (cf. 2 Cor 12:12). Transcendence is present in the body of Christ as Christ. Transcendence, however, is present likewise in individual human beings (cf. "Christ in me" Gal 2:20). The Transcendence which manifests itself as the circle (community) of human beings also works in individual human beings as the one effecting in her or him love and knowledge. In this sense we can say that Transcendence manifests itself as individual human beings. In this "manifesting itself as" we perceive the unity between Transcendence and the human. "Transcendence in me" is the Front of Transcendence which bears the being-thus of the human being and constitutes the "Self" so that the awakened human being gives expression to Transcendence in this historical reality. Here, then, we see the third type of Front-Structure (the field type).

Logos as the structural principle of the circle (*Eikon theou*) is the "content" of the working of Transcendence, the *Emeth* of God, whose incarnation is the "Self" (Christ in me, divine-human), whose activity has been designated as the "vow of Life." Here, however, we must note further: The vow of Life manifests itself indeed as my vow of Life. There is, however, between the vow of Life (*Self*) and the *Ego* both continuity and discontinuity. God indeed gives rise within me to willing, but it does not necessarily follow that I as my Ego will carry out that will (the vow of Life). The Ego is always responsible for the fulfillment. Therefore, we always had to make a distinction between the Self, which as the seat of the vow of Life is one with Transcendence, and the Ego. Transcendence in me as the Front of Transcendence constitutes the Self of the human being (Front-Structure of the field type). The Self, whose activity is the vow of Life, is structurally one with Transcendence (divine-human). The Ego, however, reflects it insofar as it realizes the will given rise to by Transcendence. In this sense we can understand here the third type of Front-Structure: Transcendence in me as the Front of Transcendence constitutes the *Self*-being of the human. The human body as the seat of the vow of Life is thereby the dwelling place of the "Holy Spirit" (cf. 1 Cor 6:19), and its life activity is identical with "Christ" (cf. Phil 1:21a). The Ego of the human being functions as the authentic Ego when the vow of Life reveals itself in the Ego so that it becomes "my vow."

Integration

The Body of Christ and Integration

In order to shift more clearly from Buddhist thinking to Christian, in this chapter we interpret our circle as a community of persons which in its essence is historical. Then it will be seen that our circle presents something Christian in contrast to something Buddhist. We have observed our circle synchronically, leading to Buddhist results. In contrast to Buddhist thinking, Christian thinking is diachronic—in a somewhat simplified expression: Christianity understands the world in the context of history, while Buddhism understands history in the context of the world. In Christian theology, above all in the Western European tradition, the focus is on the relationship between God and God's people. In Buddhism all efforts from the very beginning concentrate on the solution to the problem of being self. The motto of Zen Buddhism—to clarify the question of being self—has been the goal of Buddhism in general.

For our purposes we will introduce in this chapter a new concept: "integration." By an integrated system we understand a unified object which is constituted in several poles. We will again take the example of music. It can best serve as a likeness of the community of persons. First of all we must ask whether there is such a thing as music. If only objective things existed, things whose existence can be objectively confirmed, it would be difficult to state that "there is music." Objectively one can demonstrate that there are vibrations of the air. However, that is something other than music. Now, we are not attempting here to demonstrate the existence of music. If, however, one grants that there is music, one then already presupposes something like integration, for a piece of music is a unified object which is constituted by various poles (tones). Thus, what must first be shown here is that the tones in the music are poles. In the melody one tone is preceded by the other tones and it awaits the following tones. In the musical field one tone produces a specific phase, in which it spreads out its Front. The tone passes, but its Front remains. The next tone comes into the phase which the preceding tone had brought forth. The second tone appropriates this phase, the Front of the first tone. The second tone does not exist in isolated fashion. It is there as a musical tone in that it appropriates the Front of the first tone and is thereby qualified anew. Likewise, the first tone on its side is newly qualified in the memory of the listener by the second. There is a Front-Exchange between them. The two tones together form again a new phase, which is not simply the sum of the first and the second phases. And this latter then draws in the oncoming tone, and so forth.

The melody is a unified object. However, between the tones which constitute the melody there exists the Front-Exchange, without which the melody would be the mere sum of physical tones. The same is also true of chords, themes, and movements. When we play a piano piece, we cannot sound the first tone without having the whole piece in mind. The first and the last tones condition each other, indeed presume each other (circle). We can indeed say that every tone reflects in itself all the others, indeed not physically, but certainly musically. If we play one part more rapidly than usual, then we must play the entire piece correspondingly fast, or the other parts in contrast, more slowly. A modification in one part of the piece expands its effect forward and backward, and indeed in the manner of the nebula structure. The modification of one part causes the modification of other parts, especially in the immediately following parts, but in the end, all the parts are affected. Through the modification of every part, the first modification is justified, so to speak, and the harmony of the entire piece remains intact. That indicates that a piece of music in its structure is circular, just as it is in its inner causality, so that the tone, but also the theme and the movement, are each poles. Music, which appears to move on in linear fashion, is structurally a circle.

If one makes a mistake while playing, the observant listener notes it, although the listener does not know the notes by heart. The mistake causes a disturbance in the musical field. The tone in question loses the relationship to the other tones, which in turn has its effect on the entire piece. The mistake immediately calls forth a reaction: The integration, which was disturbed by the mistake, must be won again. This reaction is not a demand grounded in an objective perception, that the player should play according to the correct notes, but rather, so to speak, in the inner need of the musical field itself (the heart of the musician). From this we see that the musical field, the heart of the one playing the music, is a field of force in which the tones are integrated into music. The tones organize themselves within it into an integrated whole.

The relationship between the pole and the whole is easy to perceive in a concert (for example, in a quartet). Every player must play independently, but at the same time listen to fellow players and fit in with their playing. Independence and dependence belong together. Every player gives their fellow player their music with independent playing. It is the condition of the playing of the others, the background for their making music. Each one transforms the music of the fellow player into the conditions of their own playing. This is in a wider sense the Front-Exchange which everyone carries out, when one, for example, takes a walk and transforms the gravity of the earth into the condition of one's taking a walk. Every player is the center of the whole. The whole is constituted by the poles, of which each again is a center. In order to analyze this integrated system, we need a further concept: *uniting factor*. Uniting factor is that which is valid in the same measure for each constituent, that is, what is more or less normative. In music, for example, the key, but also the tempo, is the uniting factor. The uniting factor is also visible in the figure of the director. The uniting factor is something other than the integration itself. The former is a moment of the latter. The uniting factor is indispensable for integration. However, it can destroy integration, for example, if one plays the entire piece from beginning to end with a mechanically equal tempo. Then pole's freedom is lost.

Music is a likeness of the community of persons. The tone in its individuality or the concert musician in their independence and freedom is a likeness of the person. The musical piece as a whole stands for the community. The human heart as the musical field in which the tones are integrated into music and thereby express this field is an analogy of Transcendence as the field of force in which persons organize themselves into an integrated community and thereby give expression to the field of force in historical reality. Just as the heart, when it manifests itself as music, is one with the music, so also is Transcendence, in that it manifests itself as the community of the saints in historical reality, one with the community. The community of persons as the expression of Transcendence is likewise divine-human. Expressed otherwise, Transcendence "in" the community is one with it (cf. 1 Cor 12:12).

Further: Music is present if it is understood. Objectively it does not exist. If I play a piano piece which I totally do not understand, then certainly I do not play well, even if I might play the notes correctly. The tones, if they had a mouth, would say: "Stop! You are not letting us dance as we wish!" If they are played without understanding, the notes indeed are there, but the music is missing. When, on the contrary, I play the piece that I understand well, I experience at once the tones' wish: "This is how we wish to sing!" A community of the saints as the body of Christ is objectively not there, as, for example, a sociological institution. If we are awake to the vow of Life, it illuminates our lives, enlivens our activities, so that in and through us it works and manifests itself as a community. Just as making music, so also in communal life, there lies at the basis of everything the field, in which the poles are brought to integration. They are integrated under its pressure, so to speak. Nevertheless, if we are not awake to this reality, they *de facto* do not exist.

What then is the uniting factor in community? It is the continuing structure, the order, and thereby the law (including customs and morality). In the church canons, dogmas and rites belong to the uniting factors. We must add the sense of belonging to the same group or to a common tradition to this. In the state, the uniting factor is presented in the form of the state's president. In our living together, the uniting factors include language (the unequivocal) and common sense. It is clear that the differentiating intellect has its place as a uniting factor, and completely justifiably so. That means, however, because the intellect is the property of the Ego, a possible primacy of the uniting factor over the harmony of integration would mean an unjustified primacy of the Ego over the Self, and thereby an isolation of the uniting factor from integration, the separation of the Ego (the mere Ego) from the Self.

Up until now we have discussed three concepts: "pole," "uniting factor," and "integration." How is the relationship among them to be understood? Here *The Logic of the Species* by the Japanese philosopher Hajime Tanabe (1885–1962) can be of help.[38] In the critical period before the Second World War, he outlined a state doctrine in order to raise the state beyond nationalism. In this he made use of the logical concepts, "individual," "species," and "genus," giving them a sociological interpretation. His "logic of the species" was as follows: The species (community) oppresses the individuals (citizens) with its uniformity (for example, tradition), so that the individuals in their self-assertion strove against one another and against the species. The individuals must be freed from the uniformity of the species, but not to assert themselves. They all "die" in that they give up their self-assertion. The individuals' liberation from the species' power results from the self-negation of all members of the species, who nevertheless do not exist isolated from one another. Rather, they form as free, selfless persons the genus, which, according to him, the state should be.

Tanabe wanted to restrain uncontrolled nationalism. He understood, however, the self-negation of the individual in the sense of morality. Consequently, it remained within the framework of reason and did not reach the profundity of religion. The genus for overcoming nationalism could indeed also be the community of saints which stands above the nations. Tanabe, however, thought of the state of justice. Since he called it the "state of the Bodhisattvas," he gave the state a religious significance, which was contrary to his original intention of criticizing the absoluteness of the state. After the war he did penance, although during the war he had protested against nationalism as much as he could. For him, after the war to philosophize was to engage in the way of *Metanoia* (repentance).[39] Since his thinking remained within the framework of morality, and since he explicated morality with his "logic of the species," we cannot take over his "logic" without modification.

Instead of this, we will look for his underlying intention: First of all, the self-negation of individuals here should not be understood in the sense of morality, but rather should mean the death of the mere Ego, which works with the differentiating intellect. It must die in order to be called anew into existence by the workings of Transcendence. Secondly, the genus by no means may be the state, but rather must be the community of saints, the body of Christ, in which nationality is taken up and transformed. Then we have the following corresponding explanation: The genus of Tanabe corresponds to our integrated community of the saints, the species corresponds to our uniting factor, the individuals to our persons as poles. Thus, there results a chronological schema of how integration comes about: The individuals, who under the pressure of the uniting factor have lost their freedom, will be liberated from the pressure through Transcendence, and, because the liberated persons are awakened to the workings of Transcendence, they will organize themselves within Transcendence's field of force into the integrated community of saints.

Realization of the Body of Christ

Now we wish to present somewhat more concretely the process of how the human being is freed from the law and is integrated into the church as the body of Christ. The matter, however, is very complex. The integration manifests itself differently depending on how one understands the uniting factors. Here we will take the law as an example of a uniting factor, which will be representative of all the others. Human beings live "under the law." The human being, which has lost its instinct, must learn what it must do in different situations. Humans need orientation in the world. The law-oriented human being believes that the will of God is revealed in the law. They have learned it and apply it in practical situations. They wish to justify themselves before God and their fellow human beings through the works of the law. It is good to note that here, the differentiating intellect is at work, which wants to know unequivocally what should be done in a given situation. The mere Ego is thereby at work as the ultimate subject of the works of the law. The Ego, however, is conscious of itself. It observes itself and measures how far it has followed the law and which commandments it has broken. If it has followed the law, it becomes proud of itself. It looks down on those other human beings who are not capable of carrying out the work of the law (cf. Luke 18:11). Here its true concern manifests itself: The Ego, which stands in fear of its own nothingness, wants to create security for itself, and does so through the works of the law. Although it is unaware of it, under the mask of piety and justice, in reality it seeks to provide itself security. In the same measure it is alienated from life, is separated from it. For the Ego with the differentiating intellect which works with the unequivocal language, the enemy, for example, is unequivocally the enemy—that is, nothing other than something only to be hated. It knows nothing of humanity's fundamental togetherness, in which the "love of self" and the "love of neighbor" is one since the "I" becomes "I" only in the in-one-another with a "thou."

The mere Ego thinks as follows: "I am I and no other. That I love myself means fundamentally that I do not love the other. Loving the other, however, means that I do not love myself—which is impossible for me." Thus, the mere Ego wants to know nothing of love, the love which in the Front-Structure ultimately is located in the vow of Life. If nevertheless the mere Ego does love its neighbor, it does so only because of the demand of the law. Then its love is a mere act of will (moral) and is not an expression of the original vow of Life which gives rise to love in the human being. Consequently, the legalistic person with the differentiating intellect asks for a definition of neighbor (see Luke 10:2a). If the law demands the love of neighbor, then it must be unequivocally shown who the neighbor is, otherwise it would not know who should be loved. The primordial and unconditioned quality of love is something hidden to him. In the measure with which the mere Ego studies and follows the law, it affirms itself. The law is something that is holy and good in itself for it manifests the will of God to the Ego, but it then can become a means to a hidden self-affirmation of the Ego, even though it is itself completely unaware of this (cf. Rom 7:7ff.).

The matter, as said, is very complex. In our legal Ego we find three concerns: First, such an Ego can, so to speak, be a purely social Ego; it follows the law without any looking to the side for its own security or well-being. In this case the law is understood as the principle of social order. Such an Ego can conscientiously study and follow the law simply because it is its duty. Its loyalty to the law can therefore be selflessly motivated. Nevertheless, in this case the Ego is closed within itself. It has distanced itself from its "Self"—it has alienated itself. It is a pure Ego for whom the law is the only reality because it has shut itself off from all of Transcendence's "workings" in its "Self." This Ego is not the place in which life shines forth, with the result that the Ego wills what life from its deepest foundations wills. It knows only "thou shalt," but not "I will," or "I take the vow of Life." It understands itself in the end as pure intellect, not as body, which it appears for, rather, as the seat of evil drives. Such a human being desires an ordered society and works to realize it, but the law for it is the essential matter. It has no idea of what is involved in the integration of persons. For it the factor of unity (the law) is more important than integration, and therefore also the freedom of individual human beings. It is unaware that through its legalism it suppresses, indeed, destroys the integration of free persons. Thus, it lacks the sense of life.

However, legalism is usually the mask, or at least, *also* the mask, under which the mere Ego in reality searches for its own security. Here we see the second concern of the legalist Ego, namely, the Ego as *individuum*. For the Ego as *individuum* the unifying factor is its self-identity. For the differentiating intellect sees the essence of persons, as well as of things, in their self-identity which is the unifying factor in them.

The Ego understands itself, then, as something self-identical. However, since self-identity is always in danger, namely, in danger of being lost, the Ego is concerned in creating its own security. Thus, care for itself belongs to the essence of such an Ego. It finds its expression in the fact that it searches for eternal life without knowing what it really is (cf. Mark 10:17). It understands eternal life in its way as the eternally certain continuance of its self-identical existence. That is what it wishes to receive as reward for its works of the law. Such a motive can hide itself behind the legalism of a human being.

Thirdly, the human being is always in a concrete relationship with his or her fellow human beings. The mere Ego cannot escape this. Mere Egos also bind themselves together, but in such a way that the unifying factors are the bases of their community. The unifying factor is also in this case for them the central point! The agreement of interest or of goals, the common membership in the same group or in the same tradition, the common world or life view—such unifying factors are the foundation of their friendship (cf. Luke 14:26). It is in this sense that the "friend" is defined. However, in our context we should note that the law, "You should love your neighbor!" is held to be the basis of love. Persons, however, in reality are oriented toward integration by God. Transcendence, which integrates them in that it sets the individuals out in poles, is the ground of living together, in this case, of interpersonal relationships. However, for the mere Ego the unifying factor appears to be the ground of love and living together, which results in unifying, in reality, not calling forth love and convivial existence, but rather strife with those who do not share the same unifying factor. Here the love of neighbor commandment offers help, and the mere Ego transforms love into a question of morality. The love of the enemy—in the manner of the sense of Matt. 5:43f.—is here impossible and meaningless, for it does not come forth from the mere Ego, but rather from the activated Self, that is, from the original in-one-another of I and thou.

We have seen above what the absolutized unifying factor brings forth: Separation from the life borne by Transcendence, that is, from the Self as the seat of the vow of Life, which is divine-human. Now we must ask how the individual will be liberated from uniformity.

For the Ego with the differentiating intellect which works with completely unequivocal language, uniformity is the most important thing however it may be understood. Uniformity is the primary reality for such an Ego. For the Ego exists as the Ego when it knows unequivocally what it is, where it is, and what it should do. It looks for this first of all within the realm of the uniform, by means of which it understands itself and depends on itself. Such an Ego is closed up within itself. It is separated from its "Self." It does not perceive its workings. The Self, that is, Life, does not reveal itself in this Ego. The Ego depends upon itself in that it understands itself, with its differentiating intellect, as something uniform within the context of uniformity, and acts to maintain or establish uniformity. It is dependent upon uniformity in that measure. It becomes a prisoner of uniformity because it relies on itself.

That likewise means, however, that the entire person is taken prisoner by the mere Ego. Because the Ego itself relies upon uniformity, that is, it ultimately relies upon itself, and because it has distanced itself from its Self, that is, it wishes to exist by its own power, it fears that it will be annihilated if it gives up its self-reliance. Liberation from uniformity's domination is thereby liberation of the Ego from itself. That takes place when it ceases to rely directly on itself and recognizes that uniformity is only a part of its reality. The Ego's giving up of itself and its becoming open to the Self within it occur simultaneously. One can say that becoming open to the Self is conditioned by the Ego's giving up of itself, but likewise that the Ego can give itself up when the Self reveals itself in the Ego. As soon as this happens life manifests itself in the Ego so that now the vow of Life becomes the Ego's own vow. When the sole domination of the differentiating intellect is gotten rid of, reality manifests itself as it really is, in the Front-Structure which realizes itself in the "circle," and in the case of persons, in the integration of the *Communio sanctorum*.[40] Until that point, reality manifested itself as the differentiating intellect, which works with entirely unequivocal language, had constructed it. It appeared as if self-identity were the essence of things, as if the complex of reality consisted of a series of "unified" units. But now reality manifests itself in its Front-Structure with an orientation toward integration. Insofar as the differentiating intellect's construction is secondary, the reality which now manifests itself is primary, immediate. In this immediacy, the Front-Structure manifests itself (cf. the reaction of the "good" Samaritan, Luke 10:33).[41]

On the other side, the Ego is reconciled with its Self, with its corporeality as the seat of the vow of Life. We repeat here in summary fashion: Insofar as the Ego closes itself off against its Self, that is, insofar as the Self is not revealed in the Ego, the Ego does not perceive the workings of the Self within itself. To that extent, the vow of Life is not real in the human being. It is *de facto* not there in him or her. The Ego could therefore understand itself as the absolute mere Ego. When, however, the human being is awakened to the vow of Life by its revealing itself in the Ego, it becomes activated in the human being. It becomes the effectively working reality in the human being.

Both the recognition of our reality's Front-Structure and the vow of Life's activation go hand in hand to realize the integrated community. The one demands the other. Expressed in a Christian manner: "I have been crucified with Christ; it is no longer I who live, but Christ who lives in me; and the life I now live in the flesh I live by faith in the Son of God, who loved me and gave himself for me" (Gal 2:20), that is, the Christ who at the same time is present in the church as his body. Now it is the concern of the Christian who understands themselves as a member of the body of Christ to invite other human beings to the body of Christ.

The human being will become a whole person who understands themselves as a body whose organ is the Ego. If we compare a person to a ship, then the Ego ceases to wish to be captain and becomes what it really is, that is, pilot. The Ego is the place in which the vow of Life manifests itself so that through the Ego it can effectively work on historical reality. Then the Ego, which outwardly as well as inwardly experiences things "immediately," deals with the structure of reality so as to lead to integration. The human being's freedom consists in its being freed from itself so that it is freed from direct self-reliance and its consequent selfish concern, but also from unifying thinking and the consequent will to domination. Now "Christ" (the incarnate Logos) becomes the ultimate subject within a human because "Christ" constitutes a human's subjectivity in the third type's Front-Structure. The human being lives in that Life shines in him or her, that is, in that Life comes into its own. Thus he or she lives as a free person. As far as the Ego does what the Self effectively works, it is free—when the human being says: "I am doing this," then the Ego is obedient to that which is deep within it. Freedom and obedience here are one.

After we have spoken of uniformity's domination and a person's liberation from it, we turn once again to the question of integration. Since it often was indirectly spoken of, in the following I will look particularly into the connection between integration and eschatology.

We do not need to historically develop Christian eschatology here. We have in mind that at the basis of integration's realization lies "that which realizes itself" (*Emeth* of God):[42] The vow of Life has the power to realize itself. It realizes itself, however, not in such a way that the mere Ego effects something for its maintenance, so that its accomplishments are a product of its concern for itself. It realizes itself "of itself," without any meaning being given to it by the human being (cf. Mark 4:27f.). Nevertheless, it does not realize itself mechanically. The awakened human being thereto participates therein so that Transcendence is the ultimate subject of the realization: Transcendence acts through the awakened Ego. Since there must be a differentiation between the Self and the Ego, on the one hand the building of the community of God is the human being's responsibility, but on the other hand, it transcends the action of the Ego. The integration's realization is ultimately not in human hands. It is more deeply grounded.

In this regard one can say that integration comes about as an act of God. Expressed otherwise: Insofar as human beings find themselves in Transcendence's field of force, this latter effects integration in human beings, even though this might be hidden from them. If, however, several are awakened thereto, it reveals itself in them so that these human beings begin to organize the integrated community. The Transcendence which is now becoming effective in them is the Front of Transcendence in historical reality. The small group of those who give expression to Transcendence's effect on earth is the Front of the Realm of God ultimately realizing itself. Here we see the basis of present and future eschatology existing alongside one another. The Front of the transcendent-futuristic Realm of God is there in history. Its power is already present in it. We can understand the eschatology of the New Testament in this way: The Front of the coming Realm of God has broken into our history. It is there in our history as the "Reign of God."

Nevertheless, in the third type of Front-Structure, there exists between Transcendence and its visible expression on earth a discontinuity alongside continuity. The final realization of integration is factually impossible. If it nevertheless were to be brought about, the dimensional difference between the heavenly (field) and the earthly (expression) would have to be eliminated. As long as the difference remains, the expression cannot be final. Consequently, either the earthly must be transformed into the heavenly (cf. 1 Cor 15:52) or everything must be created anew as the heavenly (cf. Rev. 21:1–5). Then there will come the final integration, the Realm of God on earth.

This will come then not as the final station of human history, but rather as something transcendent which, because it brings history to a close, at the same time fulfills the original meaning of history. It comes in such a way that the old world is completely eliminated and at the same time the authentic people of God are created. The vow of Life realizes itself finally in such a way that it breaks through the products of the mere Ego. What realizes it is, like the vow of Life, divine-human: the church as the body of Christ. If, however, we imagine the final realization of integration as "cosmic," we have an eschatological picture: when the final integration takes place, all the products of the mere Ego together with the world as its dwelling place must be annihilated. The Realm of God as the final fulfillment of the integrated community comes with a new world as its location. Then the dimensional difference between the heavenly and the earthly will be eliminated. It is thus that we understand Christian eschatology as the final realization of integration. However, the dimensional difference between the invisible field and its visible expression (its Front in historical reality) will not be eliminated. In fact, the Reign of God did not thus come as Primitive Christianity expected it.

Excursus: Concerning the Absolute Claim of Christianity

The absolute claim of Christianity is grounded in the insistence that Jesus Christ alone is the revelation of God—to which the Bible bears witness—that God is revealed nowhere else outside of him. Accordingly, Jesus Christ is simply a unique, historical figure and not a universal principle which can stand in direct relationship to every time and every place. The path to the knowledge of God is exclusively through belief in Jesus Christ, and this faith is possible only there where Jesus Christ, to whom the Bible bears witness, is proclaimed in the Christian church: *Extra ecclesiam nulla salus.* From this, religion must be understood as an impossible attempt by human beings to take possession of the truth. Within this concept a dialogue of Christians with followers of other religions is uninteresting. However, this claim is no longer maintained in equal fashion by Christians everywhere.

The situation has changed. In the United States and in Japan, but also in Europe, a serious dialogue of Christians with Buddhists has begun, and indeed with the initiatory realization that the dialogue will make a new understanding of Christianity possible. In the present situation of Protestant theology in Japan, which has been greatly influenced by the theology of Karl Barth, it is time to ask how the dialogue between Christians and Buddhists is possible, and also how far this dialogue can be meaningful. Here I would like to present an example for our reflection.

Katsumi Takizawa (1909–1984), a student of Kitaro Nishida and Karl Barth, was a theologian and philosopher of religion at Kyushu University. He drew a distinction between the primary and secondary contact of God with human beings.[43] The primary contact, that is, the fact that God is with us (Immanuel), is at the foundation of every human being, completely independent of what the human being is or is not, what it has done or not, whether it is Christ or not. He likewise calls this contact the "primordial fact of Immanuel." However, although the primary contact unconditionally belongs to every human being, the human being is not always awake to this primordial fact. When, however, precisely on the basis of this primordial fact alone, one awakens to it so that one recognizes that truth, this event is called the "secondary contact of God with human beings." By this distinction Takizawa obviously stands near the fundamental view of Mahayana Buddhism, according to which every human being has the Buddha nature, on account of which someone can become an Awakened One if someone becomes awakened to this nature.

What is important is that Takizawa develops his Christology from the perspective of this distinction: According to him, Jesus is a human being who so completely realized the secondary contact between God and the human being and gave it expression that he can be the measure and the model of the second contact. However, it is not that the primary contact itself was first brought into existence by Jesus. No, he is the model of the secondary contact and in this sense, is a figure who stands *alongside* Gautama Buddha, who in his time was the first in the Indian tradition to be awakened to the primary contact. Takizawa criticizes traditional Christianity which saw in Jesus the primary contact of God with humanity and therefore did not make any distinction in Jesus between the primary and secondary contacts, with the consequence that the human being Jesus was divinized as such. Jesus, however, was a human being who stood in inseparable, unidentifiable, and irreversible relationship to Immanuel, to the primary contact of God with the human being while that primordial fact "Immanuel" is what Christianity calls "Christ"—"true God and true man."

Takizawa likewise criticized the Buddhists. With them as well, the described distinction is not strictly carried out, though not in the same sense as in Christianity. Among Buddhists there is the tendency to view *Satori* (enlightenment), which is nothing other than the realization of the secondary contact, as fundamental and decisive so that the individual experience of enlightenment has raised to the measure of all things. Nevertheless, according to Takizawa, Buddhism is the religion which stands on the same (primordial) ground as Christianity. Thus, Takizawa has shown how dialogue between Christians and Buddhists is possible and how it can be significant for both: The primordial fact of Immanuel is a common ground of both religions; therefore the absolute claim of Christianity could be given up.

In my judgment Takizawa is correct in his distinction. I cannot here justify his thesis in detail. It need only be noted that the distinction by Takizawa corresponds to the distinction made in this essay between the Self and the Ego. The Self is the divine-human, while the Ego is the place in which the divine-human is revealed. Then the Self corresponds to the "primary contact of God with the human" and the event of the revealing of the Self in the Ego corresponds to the "secondary contact of God with the human." Immediately it might be added: According to Takizawa, the primary contact belongs unconditionally to every human being. That of course is not false but needs to be more precisely articulated. The primary contact will be activated when it manifests itself in the Ego and over against the Ego. In other words, the primary contact becomes effective in the secondary contact. Both condition each other, although the secondary contact does not call forth the primary. Before the secondary contact comes into existence, the primary *de facto* is not there. If that is so, despite Takizawa, one can dare to say that the primary contact *de facto* had not existed before Jesus awakened to it—in any case, according to the Hebrew tradition—although it is not the case that the possibility of the secondary contact first arose through and in Jesus. In this sense the fourth evangelist was correct when he said: "The law was given through Moses, the grace and truth came through Jesus Christ" (John 1:17). With this correction, I agree with Takizawa. What follows from this may not then be concealed: The interpretation of the Easter event. Takizawa believes that the Easter faith means the secondary contact's development within Jesus's disciples after his death.[44] The disciples held that the primordial fact of Immanuel, which was now revealed in them, to be the Risen One. In order to make this view convincing, one would need a detailed study, which this is not the place. Here I am attempting only to illustrate the view of Takizawa, and indeed with the concepts which were given shape in this essay:[45] Jesus was a human being in whom the activated Self was given voice through his Ego.

It is the Ego that makes use of unequivocal language. In the measure, then, in which it alienates itself from the Self, understands itself in unequivocal language, it fills itself with ideas which are formed through unequivocal language so that these ideas represent the reality for the Ego. The mere Ego understands itself and orients itself through them. Such an Ego depends on the dominant viewpoints of society, but also of tradition, which are given expression in unequivocal language. The other side of that is that the Ego has lost the direct life relationship to the Self, and, like the Self is also really not activated, indeed, is *de facto* dead. This was the case with the legalistic stream of Judaism in the time of Jesus. Indeed, we can no longer ascertain how widespread it was among the Jews of that time, but as far as legalism is concerned in any case, the analysis applies. Symptomatic of this are the Pharisees, at least as they appear in the New Testament, that is, as the opponents of Jesus; they depend upon the law and do not understand Jesus in whom the unity of the I and thou, the divine and the human in the Front-Structure—the Self—had come alive. The mere Ego had died in Jesus so that he not only was free of the selfish concern for himself (Matt. 6:25ff.), but also from discriminating reckoning: For him a single sheep was not less valuable than the whole herd (Luke 15:4ff.). For Jesus, the love of self and love of neighbor were not really distinguishable from one another, but this was not on the basis of the commandments of the law, but rather because the Self is the unity of the I and the thou (see Luke 10:25ff., 30ff.). In Jesus, the activated Self was given voice through his Ego. A sign of this can be seen in the fact that Jesus understood himself as a representative of the heavenly "Son of Humanity" on Earth and indeed in such a way that at the same time he distinguished himself from him (Mark 8:38). As an empirical person he knew himself to be subordinated to God (Mark 10:18). That is, something divine-human spoke through Jesus, and as Jesus.

Jesus was conscious of this. Therefore, to the people of that time, he appeared to be an authoritative teacher, not dependent upon the law and tradition (see Mark 1:22). When Jesus said: "I, however, say to you" (Matt. 5:21ff.), he did not thereby issue a new "ethic," which is valid as a norm for the Ego. Rather, he thereby presented things as they were experienced by an activated Self, that is, what was *de facto* the case with the Self: In the Self as something divine-human, as the unity of the I and thou, there is no hatred, even if the Ego could only hate its enemy. The Self knows no lust, although the male Ego desires women (v. 28). What comes from the Self will not be determined by what other human beings do to it. It is free of that, although for the Ego, the *jus talionis* is valid (v. 38f.). For the Self, no human being is to be viewed solely as enemy (v. 44). There is the enemy for the Ego, which wishes to dominate other Egos. Jesus, of course, did not reject the law, but he was free from it, for the law is there for the human being and not the other way around. The law is not an ultimate reality, as the Ego is not an ultimate reality in face of the divine-human; the Self is above the law (cf. Mark 2:27f.).

The disciples of Jesus could not understand him during his lifetime. After his death, however, the divine-human was revealed in them: The disciples awakened to the Self. That was the event which Paul described as the revelation of the Son of God in him (that is, "in him" as well as "to him"; Gal 1:16). The disciples interpreted this event in a manner that was common in their time: as Jesus appeared and became famous—he probably appeared to the people of that time as great as or greater than his former master John the Baptist—people said: "John the Baptist has been raised from the dead; that is why these powers are at work in him" (Mark 6:14). The disciples of Jesus interpreted the event of the Self's revealing in them in this manner: "Jesus has been raised from the dead. Therefore, his powers become effective in us." They found in themselves their Self, precisely that which once appeared as Jesus and was with them. If that is true, they thus did not distinguish between an empirical human being Jesus and the divine-human, but rather identified both without distinction. The relationship between the historical Jesus and the kerygmatic Christ can, in my judgment, be best understood in this manner. The primary contact, that is, what Jesus called "the Reign of God," and, personifying it, the "Son of Humanity," is identical with the one whom the primitive community held to be the Risen Jesus, Christ the Lord, and Son of God.

That is our interpretation of the Easter event. No historical study gives information but only probability. In this excursus, then, I wished only to show that our analysis is applicable to the New Testament so that the claim of absoluteness by Christianity can be eliminated. For the empirical human being, Jesus is to be distinguished from the "primordial fact of Immanuel" and our concept of the activated Self ("Christ in me") can well be compared to the concept of Buddhahood.

Endnotes

[1] Sunyata is one of the central concepts of Buddhist thinking. Literally sunyata means emptiness, nothingness, but in Buddhist thinking it indicates the non-substantiality of all existing beings: Nothing has in itself a sufficient basis for its being. The Chinese have interpreted this concept with the Taoist concept of "nothing." The Japanese have also taken over this concept of "nothing."

[2] Keiji Nishitani, "Ku to Soku," in *Bukkyō Shiso* [Buddhist Thinking], ed. M. Saigusa, vol. 5 (Risosha, 1982), 4ff. *Ku* is the Japanese translation of sunyata.

[3] Nagarguna (ca. 150–250 CE), the founder of Mahayana Buddhist philosophy, understood the concept of *pratītyasamutpāda* as "mutual dependence and relatedness." *Soe Sogan* is the Japanese translation, which comes by way of Chinese. Concerning *pratītyasamutpāda*, see note 13.

[4] Since the English word "front," as well as the German word "Front," in differentiation from the Japanese word *Shomen* or *Zenmen*, does in fact imply hostility, I have decided in favor of the Western word. In Japanese texts, in fact, I use the Western word "front."

[5] *Soku* is also a loan word from Chinese. Originally *soku* meant "immediately," "right away." However, as the Chinese translated *rupam sunyata* in the *Prajñāpāramitāhrdaya* Sutra with *Shiki soku ze ku*, the word *soku* took on the meaning of the paradoxical identity of opposition. For the translation means: That which the closed form (*rupa*) has "is" and at the same "is not" its opposition (namely, emptiness). Concerning emptiness see below.

[6] "Baika," in *Shobo Genzo.*

[7] *Kirisutokyō no Tetsugakuteki Rikai* (Kyobunkan, 1938), ch. 3, 1.

[8] This is a fundamental experience prior to verbalization. It has been sharply conceived by Zen Buddhists. In our words unequivocal concepts are broken through where the Front-Structure shows itself as a fundamental structure in its immediacy. Then one makes use of the conceptualization which for example the identity of opposites (*soku*) adequately expresses in language. This is true above all of the relationship between the object and the subject. It shows itself as the Front-Structure in the "immediate experience." Or, the "immediate experience" is an event in which we become intuitively aware of the Front-Structure.

[9] "Slice" in this case means my "materiality," "corporeality," "spirituality," but also my being-Japanese, being-professor, etc.

[10] This is not the place to go into this problem. The following is only a brief intimation of it: "The individual image" has in itself something of the "living relationship" to a fact. However, in the case of a social image—many readers will no doubt have a social image of a Japanese person—it can happen that it will lose the living relationship to the fact and, having lost it, begin to control the thinking and behavior toward that Japanese person. In this manner the Front without a relationship to the "center of the Front" can unwarrantedly substitute for the reality.

[11] I am grateful to Shigeru Aoki, *Kotairon no hōkai to keisei* [The Collapse and formation of the doctrine of the individual]), (Sōbunsha, 1983).

[12] In both instances Paul says literally: "the non-beings," *ta me onta.*

[13] *Pratītyasamutpāda* is alongside of sunyata, another central concept of Buddhism. While sunyata negatively means that nothing has a sufficient basis of its being in itself, *pratītyasamutpāda* means positively that one event is dependent on others. One concept is implied in the statement of the other. On the contrary, substance, which is dependent only on itself, excludes both sunyata as well as *pratītyasamutpāda*. Therefore, Buddhist thought recognizes no substance. The various Buddhist schools have developed their own understanding of *pratītyasamutpāda*.

[14] For example, Masao Yamashita, "Kuno Ronrigaku," [The logic of sunyata], *Riso*, 610

(March 1984): 60f. According to Yamashita the fourfold negation of Nagarjuna means p'q = pq' = pq = p'q' = F = T, that is, a logical impossibility.

[15] The text is as according to Hajime Nakamura, *Hannya Shingyō* [*Prajñāpāramitāhrdaya* Sutra] (Iwanami Bunko, 1958), 174.

[16] One of the Mahayana Buddhist schools in China and Japan, whose founder Chi-i (Chigi) developed his doctrine on the basis of the *Saddharmapundarika* Sutra. The core of this sutra probably arose around the beginning of the Common Era in northern south India and defended the ideal of Mahayana Buddhism. The *T'ien-T'ai-tsung* was brought in the year 805 to Japan by Saicho (*Tendai-shu*) and elements of the other Buddhist schools were taken up into it.

[17] A Mahayana Buddhist school in China which systematized the thought of the *Avataṃsaka* Sutra. The first Chinese translation of the entire sutra appeared in the fifth century. The Sanskrit original, which probably stems from the first century, however, is extant only in fragments. The founders of the school were Tu-shun and Sa-t'ang (both seventh century). This school was also brought to Japan, but it did not develop as an independent school.

[18] Wilhelm Leibniz, *Monadologie*, section 7. Monads have no windows through which things can enter and exit because they are substances.

[19] If one were briefly to characterize the two streams of Japanese Zen Buddhism, then for Rinzai-Zen the experience of "awakening" is important. In order to free the disciple from objectifying thinking and to help him to awakening the master will give him paradoxical questions (*koans*), like, for example, "When hands clap one hears them. How do you hear one hand?" To this disciple must answer, in that he shows in word and deed the activity of the "Formless" (ultimate reality in Buddhism) of which in awakening he has become aware. Soto-Zen concentrates on "*Zazen*" (sitting) as the expression of Buddhahood, to which the one sitting becomes awakened through praxis.

[20] *Zento Nippon Dunka* [Zen and Japanese Culture] in Selected Works (Shunjusha, 1955), 9:31.

[21] *Logos to Lemma* (in Japanese; Iwanami, 1975).

[22] Thus, according to Cusanus, infinity (God) is neither *generans* nor *genita*. Nicholas Cusanus, *De Docta Ignorantia*, 1, 26 (*De theologia negativa*).

[23] *Bukkyō no kontei ni aru mono* [What is at the foundation of Buddhism?] (Kodansha, 1982), pp. 14ff.

[24] Paul says that for him to live is Christ. Christ is present in his life as his life. Paul understands his whole life to be borne by Christ.

[25] This concept corresponds to the Buddhist *vijnana* (in Japanese: *funbetsu*) in contrast to awakened understanding (*prajna*).

[26] Thus, the strong as well as the weak build the structures which destroy the "Front-Structure." See above for discussion.

[27] Jodo-Buddhism as an independent Buddhism arose in Japan through the founding of *Jodo-shu* by Honen (1133–1212) and *Jodo-Shins-Shu* by his disciple Shinran (1173–1262). According to the *Sukhavati* Sutra, the main portion of which arose in the middle of the first century in northwest India, Dharmakara took a vow not to attain the status of a Buddha before he had built a Pure Land in which every human being who could not attain enlightenment through his own effort would enter after death and there be enlightened, if he believed in him and called on his name. After an endlessly long period of meditation and praxis his vow was fulfilled and he became the *Tathagata* who is called Amida-Buddha (*Amitayus*: infinite life, also called *Amitabha*: unhindered light) so that the human being, whatever kind of sinner that human may be, will be saved only through faith in the Amida-Buddha. The praxis of imagining the Amida-Buddha and his Pure Land or calling on his name was carried out by Buddhists of various

Mahayana schools and brought from India over China to Japan and has developed itself into the pure doctrine of faith. In Japan the largest number of believers belongs to Jodo-Buddhism.

[28] It is apparent that here we must make a distinction between the "Ego" and the "Self," whereby it is the "Self" that is meant by "Christ in me." "Christ in me" is the authentic, final subject of the human person, is the unity of the divine and the human (see below). The distinction between the "mere" Ego and the Ego of the believer is that the "Christ in me" arises in the Ego of a believer, while this consciousness does not arise in the mere Ego. This distinction corresponds well to the distinction which C.G. Jung makes between the Ego and the Sself, and precisely in relationship to our verse cited here: C.G. Jung, *Die Beziehung zwischen dem Ich und dem Unbewussten*, in *Gesammelte Werke* [Collected Works] (Walter Verlag, 1972), 7:243. The *Vijnapti-matrata* likewise makes a similar distinction between *mano-vijnana* and *alaya-vijnana.* I mention here only this distinction although the *Vijnapti-matrata* makes finer distinctions. However, in our further discussion here I will not go into these distinctions.

[29] For the Hebrew bible concept emeth see Gottfried Quell, "Aletheia," in *Theological Dictionary of the New Testament*, Gerhard Kittel, ed. (Eerdmans, 1964), 1:232ff.; J. Petersen, *Israel* (Oxford University Press, 1954, reprint), 1–2:336ff. The concept of "that which realizes itself" in contradistinction to the Greek concept "of being" is very important for the understanding of the Bible and of Jodo-Buddhism. The concept implies that the will of God realizes itself in history in that the human person becomes conscious of the will of God which is at work in him or her and gives it expression. (cf. Phil 2:13). The work of God in the human person constitutes the "Self" (see note 28), and it both manifests itself in the Ego and over against the Ego.

[30] Daisetsu Suzuki, *Mushin to iu koto* [What self-powerlessness means], in *Suzuki Daisetsu senshu* [Selected Works of Daisetsu Suzuki] (Shunjusha, 1955), 10:146ff. Here Suzuki discusses how an apple tree grows and bears fruit in a way which very much reminds us of Mark 4:26–29.

[31] That the vow of Life is the concern of the Self ("Christ in me"), that is, something divine-human, we will see in the following. Here, however, it should be noted that the vow of Life in our sense transcends the individual Ego and the individual Self and that the human person who is awakened to it sees in it Transcendence at work so the person can say: "Love is from God and everyone who loves is begotten of God and knows God" (1 John 4:7).

[32] See *ibid.*

[33] *Rinzairoku* (Words and deeds of Lin-chi. The oldest text we have stems from the twelfth century), "Jishu" 1.

[34] Here lies a difficult problem. We have seen how the individual exists as a pole in a circle, how the whole circle and the individuals condition each other. The individual exists as the individual in that it reflects in itself other individuals and the whole circle: There is a trans-individuality in each individual. On the other hand, the individual is aware that Transcendence is at work in him. We can make a distinction between trans-individuality and Transcendence and say that Buddhism as a whole speaks rather of trans-individuality (*pratītyasamutpāda*), while Christianity speaks almost exclusively of Transcendence. The difficulty lies in the question, how much are we in need of the concept of Transcendence; is the concept of trans-individuality not sufficient for the understanding of human life? For the latter is also confirmable by objective experience. We cannot, however, discuss this problem within the framework of this book. We do, however, wish to point out that Buddhists likewise know Transcendence (the "Formless," with Amida-Buddha as its expression). In both cases trans-individuality or *pratītyasamutpāda* as such is borne by Transcendence. In any case, we can more closely define the Self

with our concepts. The Self in distinction from the Ego is "trans-individual" on the basis of its circular Front-Structure, while it is divine-human on the basis of the Front-Structure with Transcendence.

[35] Karl Barth, *Kirchliche Dogmatik*, I/1, pp. 311ff., analyzes the concept of revelation and shows the triune nature of the one revealing, revelation, and the revealing. This corresponds to our analysis of effecting, which is manifest in the triune nature of the "agent of effecting," the "content of the effecting" and the "transmission of the effecting."

[36] Cf. John 1:3; 1:16f.; 2 Cor 3:18. The Son of God is the invisible structural principle on the basis of which the world and human beings are formed because they reflect it in themselves.

[37] A strict differentiation should be made between the eternal *Logos* (Son of God) and the incarnate one (Christ, divine-human—cf. John 1:14: becoming *flesh*, not becoming *human*). This is not immediately "Jesus," but rather, "Christ in me" (Gal 2:19)—according to our concept of the Self in distinction to the Ego (see note 28). We distinguish in the person of Jesus between the divine-human (Self) and his empirical Ego (see the Excursus below). Christ as divine-human, however, is also present in the church as the body of Christ (1 Cor 12). Then the field of force as the foundation of the "Body of Christ" is triune: The ultimate agent of the effecting (God the Father), the content of the effecting (not Jesus, but rather, the eternal *Logos*) and the transmitter of the effecting (the Holy Spirit, who leads to the awakening). Here it should be recalled once again that the Self (divine-human) becomes real, or is activated, when the human being becomes aware of it, or when it manifests itself in the Ego and over-against the Ego. The awakening and the manifesting of itself are the two sides of one and the same thing. Our distinction, *Logos*-Christ-Jesus, corresponds to the Buddhist *tri-kaya* theory: *dharmakaya* (the Formless itself); *sambhogakaya* or *ypayakaya* (e.g., Amida Buddha); *nirmanakaya* (e.g., Gautama). But in Buddhism there is no strict counterpart to the Christian dogma of the Trinity.

[38] Hajime Tanabe was a student of Kitaro Nishida, professor of philosophy at Kyoto University (1919–1945). Concerning Tanabe's philosophy see below. In the last years of his life he attempted to take up into his philosophy the moments of truth of Christianity in that he confessed himself to be "an incohative Christian." Cf. *Kirisutokyō no Bensho* [Apologetic for Christianity] in *Tanabe Hajime zenshū* [Hajime Tanabe Complete Works], (Chikuma, 1948), 10:260.

[39] Hajime Tanabe, *Zangedō toshite no Tetsugaku* [Philosophy as the way of *metanoia*] (Iwanami Shoten, 1946).

[40] While Buddhists see the existing Front-Structure, for Christians integration is something which is in the process of realizing itself but is not yet realized. Herein lies the ground for the Christian sense of history and responsibility.

[41] The works of the law, insofar as they come from the law-determined Ego, are secondary in comparison to "having mercy." What is to be noted is that in this parable the Samaritan has mercy upon a Jew, that is, upon a man who is supposed to be his enemy. That one can have a natural mercy upon an enemy is a paradox to the differentiating intellect. This paradoxical naturalness (immediacy) flows from the depth where the Self according to its structure (Front-Structure) seeks integration and therefore reacts to the breach of integration (a man lying there half dead).

[42] Cf. above note 29. Eschatology is not understandable if one does not realize the significance of self-realization on the basis of the will of God.

[43] Katsumi Takizawa, *Bukkyō to Kirisutokyō* [Buddhism and Christianity] (Hozokan, 1964), pp. 79ff. His lectures and following discussions were published in Seiichi Yagi, "The First Conference of *Tozai Shukyo Koryu Gakkai*," [Japan Chapter of East-West Relations] *Buddhist-Christian Studies* 3 (1983) 119.

[44] Katsumi Takizawa, *Seisho no Iesu to Gendai no Shii* [(The Biblical Jesus and modern thinking]) (Shinkyo Shuppansha, 1965), pp. 51f.

[45] The following is a very brief, abbreviated, presentation of my view concerning the rise of the Easter belief, which I discussed in detail in my works: *Shinyaku Shisō no Seiritsu* [The rise of New Testament belief] (Shinkyo Shuppansha, 1963); *Kirisuto to Iesu* [Christ and Jesus] (Kodansha, 1979); *Bukkyō to Kirisutokyō no Setten* [The contact point between Buddhism and Christianity] (Hozokan, 1975); *Paulo-Shinran, Iesu-Zen* [Paul-Shinran, Jesus-Zen])(Hozokan, 1983).

PART TWO

A Jerusalem-Tokyo Bridge

Buddhist-Christian Dialogue and the Thought of Seiichi Yagi

by

Leonard Swidler

What is Dialogue?

It is a long way from Jerusalem to Tokyo, spiritually as well as physically. Spiritually here I mean from the religion of Jesus the Jew and his followers to the religion of Gautama the Indian, and in particular to Japanese Zen Buddhism. In the past there have been physical encounters, but on the spiritual level we Christians and Buddhists have tended either simply to ignore each other, or shout, or even throw things, at the other (the latter two have been almost exclusively "Christian" activities). The other spiritual possibility, to "visit" each other, had been avoided—if it ever had even been thought about. But, to make the journey in either direction a reliable bridge would have to be erected, a bridge of dialogue.

In fact, a kind of footbridge has already been set up and a number of venturesome individuals have gone forth over it—and come back with stirring, stimulating news of the Other. As a result more have set about to expand the narrow footbridge to something broader that will bear heavier traffic, for more and more travelers are being attracted by what they hear of the Other, and, even more fundamentally, by the ever-pressing human search for Truth. What is this bridge called dialogue?

A Description of Dialogue

When we talk of dialogue today we mean an intellectual, spiritual encounter between two or more persons or groups that is different from what these encounters usually have been in the past. In the past they were confrontation, argument, debate, subjection, convert-making, or the like. In brief, each of us came to the encounter from a position of assumed superiority; we came not to learn but to teach—because we had the truth, and to the extent the others differed from us they were in error: Such, in large measure, has been the history of the past encounters between religions and ideologies.[1] That, however, is not what is meant today by dialogue.

Rather, dialogue is an encounter between two or more persons or groups of differing views with the primary purpose of learning, not teaching. I come to dialogue with my partner not from a position of assumed superiority in the matter under discussion, but rather I come as one who hopes to learn from my partner, and change, reorder my life accordingly. Precisely here is the essential difference between dialogue and all other types of intellectual, spiritual encounters.

Of course, if I am to learn, my partner has to teach, has to explain as clearly as possible their understanding of the matter at hand. When that is done effectively, at the very least I will have learned accurately what my partner thinks on a subject, which will replace the ignorance, or distortion, I had earlier. It is also possible that some of the things I hear from my partner will be new to me, and I will have learned thereby. It is even possible that my partner's explanation of a matter will be so cogent that I will be led to modify, or even reject, an earlier held position of my own—because I am convinced that I thereby have a greater grasp of reality, of truth. The latter result is, from all experience, very rare, but I must be open to the possibility if I enter into dialogue, for that is precisely the purpose of dialogue, to learn, to attain a fuller, clearer grasp of reality, of truth, and change and live my life accordingly.

There is, then, a risk in dialogue: We might have to change, and to change demands psychic energy. For the law of inertia operates in the spiritual sphere as well as in the physical: "A body at rest tends to remain at rest and a body in motion tends to remain in motion." Just as a physical body at rest or moving in a certain direction and speed can be brought into motion or deflected onto another course only by the expenditure of physical energy in some form, so too a firmly held intellectual notion can be moved or modified only with the expenditure of spiritual energy. We will not simply be able to assert, but will have to think anew. And thinking takes energy, a great deal of energy! We will have to remove ourselves from our comfortable resting place and move in a new direction. We will have to fight against the psychic law of inertia.

Put in other terms: It appears clear to me that the Capital Sin of human beings is not pride, as has often been claimed in the past, but sloth, laziness. It is easier to remain at rest where we are intellectually, spiritually. A decision not to exert the energy needed to gain a better insight into reality, probably very early in a chain of events and decisions, is, in my judgment, the fundamental essence of that old-fashioned notion of "sin." Socrates and Hinduism were moving in this same direction when the former maintained that the essence of moral evil is ignorance, and the latter the fundamental human evil as the lack of knowledge vidya, that is, avidya. I would rather say that the root of moral evil is the decision at a critical point not to exert the energy needed to come to a better knowledge on which to base one's moral decisions—laziness, inertia.

If I am at all near the mark, perhaps this is one reason why it has taken humankind so many thousands of years to begin to accept the risk of dialogue. It demands so much energy to think our way through the new, to overcome the fear of the unknown.

But now that some have seen how great the rewards of dialogue are, how much more surely, quickly and deeply one comes to an ever-fuller grasp of reality, of truth, through dialogue, more and more individuals and even whole groups and communities are attracted to it.

Guidelines for Interreligious Dialogue

Elsewhere I have written about the rules that have to be observed if full authentic dialogue is in fact to occur.[2] In fact, the most critical ones are implicit in the very definition of dialogue, but they are too important to leave unarticulated here, at least briefly:

1. Clearly in the first encounters between individuals or communities, the most difficult points of differences should not be tackled. Rather, those subjects which give promise of highlighting commonalities should be treated first so mutual trust between the partners can be established and developed. For without mutual trust there will be no dialogue.
2. Essential to the development of this needed mutual trust is that each partner come to the dialogue with total sincerity and honesty. In dialogue my partner wishes to learn to know me and my tradition as we truly are; this is impossible, however, if I am not totally sincere and honest. The same is true for my partner, of course; I cannot learn to know them and their traditions truly if they're not completely sincere and honest. Note also, that we must simultaneously presume total sincerity and honesty in our partner as well as practice them ourselves, otherwise there will be no trust—and without trust there will be no dialogue.
3. In dialogue care must also be taken to compare our ideals with our partner's ideals and our practices with our partner's practices. If we compare our ideals with our partner's practices we will always "win," but of course we will learn nothing—a total defeat of the purpose of dialogue.
4. Each partner in the dialogue must define her or himself; only a Muslim, for example, can know from the inside what it means to be a Muslim,

and this self-understanding will change, grow, expand, deepen as the dialogue develops, and hence perforce can be accurately described only by the one experiencing the living, growing religious reality.

5. Each partner should come to the dialogue with no fixed assumptions as to where the authentic differences between the traditions are, but only after following the partner with sympathy and agreement as far as one can without violating one's own integrity will the true point of difference be determined.
6. Only equals can engage in full authentic dialogue; the degree of inequality will determine the degree of two-way communication, that is, the degree of dialogue experienced.
7. A major means of dialogue is a self-critical attitude toward ourself and our tradition. If we are not willing to take a self-critical look at our own, and our tradition's, position on a subject, the implication clearly is that we have nothing to learn from our partner—but if that is the case we are not interested in dialogue, whose whole purpose is to learn from our partner. To be sure, we come to the dialogue as a Buddhist, as a Christian, as a Marxist, etc., with sincerity, honesty and integrity. However, self-criticism does not mean a lack of sincerity, honesty, integrity. In fact, a lack of self-criticism will mean there is no valid sincerity, no true honesty, no authentic integrity.
8. In the end, the most fundamental means to dialogue is having a correct understanding of dialogue, which is a two-way communication so that both partners can learn from each other, and change accordingly. If this basic goal is kept firmly in view and acted on with imagination, then creative, fruitful dialogue, and a growing transformation of each participant's life and that of their communities will follow.

We are here talking about a quite specific kind of dialogue, an interreligious/interideological dialogue. This is a dialogue between two or more persons who understand themselves to be members of differing religious or ideological traditions. It is obvious that persons not adherents of any religion or ideology can enter into very authentic and fruitful dialogues on religious or ideological matters; they would be called religious/ideological dialogues, but they would not be called interreligious/interideological dialogues.

Who then counts as a Catholic, a Jew, a Buddhist, etc.? If we are speaking of official dialogues, then of course the appropriate official will have to designate the community's representatives, but in the vast majority of cases, the dialogues will not be official. Then each person must decide for themselves whether to adhere to a particular tradition. Moreover, if the dialogue indeed is to be interreligious or interideological, then it must also be a two-sided dialogue—on the one side with the partner across the faith line, and on the other with one's *confrères/consoeurs*. Only thus will the larger community share in the fruits of the dialogue, gain in knowledge and be able to change accordingly.

If the dialogue with one's own co-religionists does not continue apace, the dialogist runs the danger of eventually becoming a tertium quid (third something)—a Buddhist, Muslim, or Hindu who no longer feels at home in any kind of Buddhism, Islam or Hinduism—so that rather than building a bridge between two isolated groups, the dialogist will form a third isolated group—hardly one of the goals of dialogue!

The Japanese Christian theologian Seiichi Yagi has in fact meticulously been building a bridge of dialogue between Buddhism and Christianity, but of course he has not been alone in this project.

Buddhist-Christian Dialogue

From the very beginning of Christianity there has been a range of fascinating historical encounters between Buddhism and Christianity in a variety of ways. Some contemporary Christian scholars see definite Buddhist influences in the New Testament.[3] Even more stunning in a way is the fact that later Gautama Buddha even turns up in Christian tradition as a Christian saint, Saint Jehosaphat, although of course the Christians were not, and still for the most part are not, aware of the fact.

Wilfred Cantwell Smith carefully traces the fantastic journey of the story of the Great Renunciation by the Indian Prince, who in fact was Siddhartha Gautama, the Buddha, into becoming the Christian saint Josaphat. Shortly before the beginning of this century Leon Tolstoy was moved to a religious conversion of life by the story of Saint Josaphat and Saint Barlaam, the former being the Great Renouncer and the latter his converter. The story came into Western European languages from a Christian Greek version, which was based on a prior eleventh-century Christian Georgian one. That in turn, however, was based on an Arabic Muslim version, which itself was taken from a still prior Manichee version. But the trail did not end there, for the original came from a second to fourth-century Sanskrit Mahayana Buddhist original.

Among other things, Smith noted that in the story Gautama (or "Josaphat") was not yet a Buddha, but rather a future Buddha, that is, a Bodhisattva. In the Manichee versions that term appears as "Bodisaf," in the Arabic version as "Yudasaf," in the Georgian as "Iodasaph," in the Greek as "Ioasaph," and in the Latin as "Josaphat." Thus, Gautama the Buddha arrived at Manichee, Muslim and Christian sainthood. As we said when I was a boy: "Jumping Jehosaphat!"[4]

Although Buddhism in general tends to be quite tolerant (one must be careful, however, not to romanticize its tolerance, for Buddhists too can also exhibit varieties of arrogance), Christianity in general, until recent decades, has tended to be very polemic and imperial in its attitude toward other religions, including, of course, Buddhism. However, that imperious Christian attitude has been changing dramatically in the last two or three decades. This is specifically also quite true of the Christian attitude toward Buddhism. Since the end of World War II, and more especially since the end of Vatican Council II (1962–65), more and more Christians have reached out in dialogue and cooperation toward Buddhists.

Organization of the Dialogue

These dialogues are taking place on many levels and in many places, so much so that it would be an impossible task to chronicle them all, either here or elsewhere. Nevertheless, it should be noted that they have reached an increasing level of organized form, and that some of the salient events are as follows (perceived somewhat from a myopic North American view):

The University of Hawaii Religion Department organized an "East-West Religions Project," out of which flowed the first International Buddhist-Christian Conference, held in 1980; the following year a journal, Buddhist-Christian Studies, was begun by David Chappell; in 1982 a "Japan Chapter of the East-West Religions Project" was launched by Masotoshi Doi; in 1983 a North American Buddhist-Christian Theological Encounter Group (in many ways a misnomer since the invited participants include not only North Americans, but also Europeans and Asians) was started by John Cobb and Masao Abe—although only about twenty-five invited theologians are active participants, at its 1986 meeting, for example, over 200 additional auditors attended as well;[5] in 1984 a Second International Buddhist-Christian Conference was held; in 1987 a Third International Buddhist-Christian Conference was held—it, for example, had over 700 registered participants and 200 presenters (who produced over 3,000 pages of scholarly papers!) and at times 1,500 listeners attended the lectures;[6] also in 1987 a new "Society for Buddhist-Christian Studies" was formed (and in "sympathetic vibration" the "Japan Chapter of the East-West Religions Project" changed its name to the "Japan Society for Buddhist-Christian Studies"). This new society obviously has an initial American base, but is international in its orientation and scope, even membership, and hopes also to become even more so in membership and affiliation.[7]

Areas of the Dialogue

There are three main areas of contact and dialogue occurring between Buddhists and Christians: 1) the intellectual, theological sphere; 2) cross stimulus and cooperation in social justice issues; 3) Buddhist and Christian monastic and spiritual life.

There is a growing flood of articles and books dealing with various aspects of Buddhist-Christian dialogue appearing in a number of languages. Probably the most comprehensive, though of course not total, coverage is to be found in the Book Review and Ecumenical Abstracts sections of the quarterly, the Journal of Ecumenical Studies. Besides the printed materials, there is an increasing number of dialogic meetings of all kinds between Buddhist and Christian scholars and leaders. Sometimes these take place within the context of formal organizations, like some of those already mentioned, or the Sunyata and Kenosis Group or the Religion and Healing Group, sometimes within the context of permanent interreligious dialogue centers, like the Nanzan Institute in Nagoya, Japan, and sometimes on an ad hoc basis.

Christian and Buddhist agencies around the world committed to social justice issues increasingly find themselves cooperating for the sake of greater effectiveness. This area too has been fruitful in spawning specific groups which are either activist or reflective on activism, such as the Liberation Theology and Buddhism Group, the Women in Buddhism and Christianity Group, and the Korean Minjung Theology and Buddhism Group.

There has been a great deal of exchange between monks, and some nuns, from both the Buddhist and Christian sides, with individuals or groups from one side living in the monasteries of the other side and participating in their life as fully as possible. These efforts have now also been organized on an international level into a Monastic and Contemplative Group. In addition, institutions like the Naropa Institute in Boulder, Colorado have for years been holding annual Christian and Buddhist Meditation Conferences, which also draw hundreds of participants.[8]

Topics in the Dialogue

Simply from some of the major aspects of Buddhism and Christianity themselves, a wide range of potential topics for dialogue between Buddhism and Christianity become apparent, many of which have in fact already consciously been more or less pursued by Buddhists and Christians in dialogic fashion. Here I wish to take up ever so briefly several which I believe offer some of the most creative possibilities for dialogue.

a) Gautama the Buddha's Basic Teaching

For Christians there are a number of critical topics for dialogue with Buddhism in the fundamental teachings of Buddhism itself. Buddhism, which takes its name from a title given to its founder—Buddha, the Enlightened One—stems from the fifth-century BCE. Siddhartha Gautama. His teaching and life's example lie at the foundation of what has come to be called Buddhism. As a young man he was led to seek a deeper meaning of life than that of luxury, and started by several years of severe asceticism. This did not bring him to the goal he desired, and so he tried the route of meditation, and thereby found Enlightenment, existential insight into the meaning of life. Since his way to Enlightenment was neither that of luxury nor severe asceticism, he often referred to it as the Middle Way—perhaps not unlike that ethical saying of that Western philosopher Aristotle: In medio stat virtus (In the middle stands virtue).

At the heart of Gautama's teaching are his so-called Four Noble Truths. It is important for Christians, and Westerners in general, to note carefully that this teaching is not world-fleeing or pessimistic, but rather "realistic":

1. At the core of life there lies dukkha (in Sanskrit), suffering; even in the midst of joy and ecstasy there is the fact that "this too shall pass." Death lies at the end of the road of every human life, and the awareness of that sooner or later forces its way through; that is dukkha. All joy, and sorrow, like earthly life in general, is impermanent, and to lead an authentic life this fact must be faced and accepted.
2. The fundamental cause of dukkha is tanha (in Sanskrit), clinging, sometimes translated as "desire." The latter translation, however, is not only not accurate, but misleading. It is not the existence of desire as such that causes dukkha, for then life and dukkha would be synonymous, since life by definition includes movement and there would be no movement if there were no energy or force to bring it about. As our very language tells us, if there is a lack of a "motivating force" there will be no movement, and a total lack of movement means death, the lack of life. But "desire" is just another name for "motivating force." Rather, it is the "clinging," which more accurately expresses the meaning of tanha, to the desired goal, the not wanting to "let go" that is the cause of the dukkha,

the suffering (note, the "goal" might also be negative, that is, the desire to avoid something).

3. The third Noble Truth is arrived at by simple deductive reasoning, that is, the elimination of a cause eliminates its effect. Therefore, the elimination of tanha will lead to the elimination of dukkha.
4. Tanha can in fact be eliminated, namely, by following Gautama's Eightfold Path, a series of methodological cognitive/ethical rules of right thinking and acting. They are: I, Right Understanding; II, Right Thought; III, Right Speech; IV, Right Action; V, Right Livelihood; VI, Right Effort; VII, Right Mindfulness; VIII, Right Concentration.

Note, these are not doctrines but rather, as said, methodological rules of how to think and act. Hinduism, out of which Buddhism sprang, already had a plethora of doctrines, myths, scriptures and the like. Gautama did not condemn them, nor did he particularly embrace them. He saw himself, rather, as a kind of very practical physician of the soul—quite like Jesus in that—who, as such, was disinterested in what he understood as speculative questions. Hence, there is the famous parable of his wherein he tells of a person who while walking through the woods was struck by a poisoned arrow. Rather than insisting first on learning whence the arrow came, who shot it, to what end, etc.—all very interesting speculative questions—the person, according to Gautama, should remove the arrow [i.e., tanha] as quickly as possible; waiting for the answers to the speculative questions [God and other metaphysical issues] might well prove fatal [i.e., dukkha].

Gautama used the term nirvana to designate the goal of human life. Nirvana literally means "blown out," basically meaning that tanha and the false self (Atman, self, in Sanskrit and Atta in Pali) has been "blown out" from the person—thus leading to the Buddhist doctrine of Anatta, No-Self. Although there is the tradition in Buddhism of understanding Anatta ontologically, that is, that there is "no-soul" in the human being, there is also a more psychological understanding, that is, the self that appears on the surface, such as that of the senses, desire for power, pride, etc., or even the successive layers underneath, is not the authentic self; in fact, the authentic self is a never-ending project, an open-ended movement toward an ever-receding horizon, toward a fullness that is never completed—a constant growth toward that which Christians and others call the infinite God.

b) Theism, Atheism, Non-Theism

Hence, for Gautama the question of gods or God was fundamentally a speculative question which did not draw his interest, probably, as mentioned before, because there was already a myriad of divinities and speculations in the Hinduism of his time and he experienced them as distractions rather than directions on the path to Enlightenment. As a consequence, his teaching can most accurately be described as non-theist rather than a-theist, and certainly not anti-theist.

But even after Gautama "had pulled the arrow out" there was still a basic reason that he and his first followers tended not to speak of gods or God; it was a matter of thought categories. God-talk in the beginning of human history naturally tended to be anthropomorphic, more precisely speaking, gynomorphic, and then only later, andromorphic. This was true in most cultures.

When, however, humankind began to move beyond this kind of concrete "picture" thought and language to a more abstract pattern, the philosophical categories developed tended to be substance categories, as for example, preeminently Platonist and Aristotelian god-speculation first in Hellenism and then in Judaism, Christianity, and Islam. The situation had been similar in Gautama's India, but his thought categories were different; instead of substantive they were relational. However, not to use substance thought categories also incurred not speaking of gods or God, who had been thought and spoken of only in substance categories.

c) Relational Process Thinking

Here we come to the key Buddhist concept of "dependent co-origination" (*pratītyasamutpāda* in Sanskrit), meaning that all things are causally interrelated. No thing exists isolated, by itself, but rather all things exist as networks of interrelated connections and causes.[9] Recalling that a classical definition of substance is "a being whose 'to be' is not to be in another," Gautama's "relational" way of thinking clearly was other than the substance way of thinking.

There is in it, however, a certain resemblance to some philosophical strands in the Western tradition, starting with some of the Pre-Socratic Greek thinkers, particularly Heraclitus, a near-contemporary of Gautama who saw all reality ultimately as "becoming," and then much later in the nineteenth century to the "dynamic" philosophers like Fichte, Schelling and Hegel, but most of all to twentieth-century process thinkers: Maurice

Blondel, Henri Bergson, Franz Rosenzweig, Pierre Teilhard de Chardin, and especially Alfred North Whitehead, and the Christian theologians who have been influenced by them.

Thinking in relational, process philosophical categories, however, does not necessarily mean the thinker must be non-theist. Whitehead and many of the above-named relational process thinkers clearly were theists, though in many ways of a quite different sort than many of their Western predecessors. Nevertheless, thinking in relational process categories makes it more possible to operate in a non-theistic mode. For example, in such a thought world the notion of a Supreme Being could never occur. Coupling this potentiality with the already mentioned "distracting" quality of the "god-talk" of Gautama's day, provides the basic reasons, I believe, for early Buddhist avoidance of theism.

Thus, we have two major models or paradigms of thought categories: one, the substance paradigm which stresses permanence, being and separateness; and two, the relational paradigm which stresses transiency, becoming and relatedness. The first has tended to be dominant in traditional Christian thought, although the relational strand also was present to a minor degree stemming from biblical thought and some Pre-Socratic thought, and recently much more strongly flowing from the "dynamic" philosophers and theologians. The second has tended to be dominant throughout Buddhist thought, although the first is popular in Buddhist-influenced cultures, and also surfaces in a number of ways among their thinkers, often not well integrated into their relational thought patterns, but nevertheless there.

Must one make a choice? Yes, and no, I believe. In our everyday life we inevitably think and act within the substance paradigm. But at the level of philosophical reflection the modern Western "dynamic" thinkers have disclosed insights into how to perceive reality that more and more Western thinkers are finding compelling—and this is true in the physical sciences as well as in the more abstract philosophical disciplines. Newtonian physics is certainly the paradigm within which all our ordinary physics thought and action occurs, but beyond the level of building bridges, buildings, and the like, what physicist can today dispense with Einsteinian relativity thinking? Physicists today, however, are still forced to think in alternating patterns, perceiving matter on the one hand as corpuscular and on the other as wave-like. As they strive for an integrated model, so too present-day philosophical thinkers, while being forced more and more to think in alternating patterns, substance and relational, must strive for an integrated model. It is precisely here that typical Christian and Buddhist thought patterns can help one another.

Paul Ingram makes a similar point:[10]

> Both may be true reflections of reality … both paradigms express differing yet valid interpretations of the bipolar structure of the experience of self identity though time. … The Buddhist non self paradigm overstresses the experience of becoming at the expense of ignoring the experience of stability and permanency by explaining it away as a delusion, and the Christian self-paradigm overstresses the experience of permanence and stability while ignoring the experience of becoming. … A more integrative interpretation of the relationship than either the traditional Buddhist non self paradigm or the traditional Christian self paradigm seems capable of developing separately.

d) Ultimate Reality

This of course in no way means that Gautama or early Buddhism had no notion of Ultimate Reality or of the Transcendent. They did, but it was conceived in their relational process categories. Ultimate Reality was thought of something like the fundamental relational, processive structure of all reality. (I say, "something like" because the very form of our language almost unconsciously leads us in the direction of substance thinking, as when I spoke of the "structure of all reality." We must be extremely cautious with our use of language, especially in such abstract matters, and not unwittingly let it lead us into affirming something we do not really intend.) I also used the term Transcendent in connection with Gautama and early Buddhism. This is meant literally, namely, that which "goes beyond" the everyday experience of life, of reality—but of course not understood in substance categories but in relational process ones.

This understanding of Ultimate Reality, of the Transcendent, is obviously a non-personal understanding, whereas the term theism means precisely belief in a god who is personal. But, of course not all the great Hellenistic, Jewish, Christian, and Muslim thinkers have always thought and spoke of Ultimate Reality, the Transcendent, only in personal terms. Notions like Thomas Aquinas's Uncaused Cause or Unmoved Mover, as only one example, are cast in non-personal philosophical categories. Hence, speaking of Ultimate Reality, the Transcendent, in non-personal categories at least some of the time does not exclude the possibility of also utilizing personal categories in speaking of Ultimate Reality, the Transcendent.

Nevertheless, it was in the non-theistic, non-personal, relational process mode of thought that Gautama and early Buddhism thought and taught, with the result that in speaking of Ultimate Reality, the Transcendent, they developed the key concept of Ultimate Reality being "emptiness," sunyata.

Exactly what is understood by sunyata needs to be probed. It can be said that emptiness is another name for the Buddhist doctrine of *pratītyasamutpāda*, dependent co-origination, which, as noted above, in short means that nothing exists as a self-subsisting, isolated thing; rather, everything is ultimately a net of relationships, and consequently is always in flux, is "becoming." It was the second century CE Nagarjuna, the second patriarch of Mahayana Buddhism—more about that below—who developed the doctrine of sunyata. He clearly denied that there are any self-subsisting substances, but insisted that whatever "is" at any moment of space time consists of conditions or relationships, and these too are dependently co-originated: "The 'originating dependently' we call 'emptiness.'" "Emptiness is dependent co-origination" (cited in Ingram). Thus, sunyata does not mean simply the lack of everything, but rather has the quite positive meaning of being the Ultimate Source of all reality, and its, sunyata's, very "nature" is that of unspecified relatedness in process.

The Zen Buddhist of the Kyoto school, Masao Abe,[11] in recently attempting to build a bridge between the theistic notion of "God" and Buddhist notion of "sunyata," made use of the Mahayana doctrine of the threefold body, the trikaya, of the Buddha, that is, of Ultimate Reality. In this doctrine the three bodies are named, first, the manifestation body, nirmanakaya, second, the heavenly body, sambhogakaya, and third, dharmakaya, in ascending order, as it were. According to Abe, the nirmanakaya is like the various human manifestations of Ultimate Reality, e.g., Moses, Jesus, Gautama, Mohammed. The sambhogakaya is like the several personal Gods affirmed by the various traditions, e.g., Yahweh, the Holy Trinity, Allah, Ishvara (of Hinduism), Amida (of Pure Land Buddhism), who have various virtues, characteristics, names, etc. At the highest point is Ultimate Reality itself, dharmakaya, which Abe describes as "formless Emptiness or boundless Openness."

In many ways this suggestion is reminiscent of comparisons that have been made between the Semitic and Hindu notions of the ultimate. On the Hindu side there is the distinction between Brahman without attributes (Nirguna Brahman) and Brahman with attributes (Saguna Brahman, later identified with Ishvara), and on the Semitic side there are the various expressions of the distinction between God in se (e.g., Yahweh, Elohim, Hebrew names for God as such) and God ad extra (e.g., Ruach or Spirit, and Hohmah or Wisdom). Thus, it would seem that the Semitic, Hindu, and Buddhist notions of Ultimate Reality are similar at least in that they all affirm that the Ultimate is boundless, infinite, unutterable in itself, and that various aspects of it are encountered, perceived by humans. The Christian John Hick, in commenting favorably on Abe's suggestion, likens this distinction to that of Kant's distinction between the noumenon, the thing in itself, which we do not perceive, and the phenomena, which we do.[12]

It is not difficult for thinkers of the Semitic religious traditions and the theistic strand of the Hindu traditions to accept a theologia negativa, an apophatic theology that acknowledges that the grandest proclamations about God are like whispers in the face of the Infinite Hurricane. It is true that the theistic traditions would tend to speak of God more in terms of Pure Act, Pleroma, Fullness, rather than Pure Potency, sunyata, emptiness. However, there might not be the contradiction involved here which appears to exist on the surface, for just as the theistic notion of God as Pure Being (Actus Purus) is conceived as the very opposite of stasis, namely, as dynamis, so also the non-theist notion of the Ultimate, namely, Nothingness, das nichts, emptiness, sunyata, is also thought of not in static but dynamic terms:

> This Emptiness is not a static state of emptiness, but rather a dynamic activity constantly emptying everything including itself. It is formless formlessness, takes various forms deeply by negating its own formlessness. This is the reason that "Formless Emptiness" or "Boundless Openness" is here regarded as the ultimate ground which dynamically reveals itself both in terms of personal "Gods" and in terms of "Lords" that are historical religious figures.[13]

Where a more serious difficulty does arise, however, is in the fact that the theist tradition is reluctant to give up the affirmation that Ultimate Reality is ultimately personal and accept that it is "Formless Emptiness" in the sense that negates, or even goes beyond, the personal in a way that obviates it. The Hindu Sengupta probably speaks for the theistic tradition in general when he writes: "In the upanishadic view there is no negation of the personality of the ultimate. There is no need for the Transcendence of personality, for the personality, which the ultimate is, is free from the limitations of human personality."[14]

Perhaps a resolution of the apparent contradiction lies in an analysis of how the human mind and language works. When theists state that the Ultimate is personal they mean to affirm something positive about it. But by the very fact of making an affirmation, the theist necessarily asserts certain limitations, even when immediately rushing in with a: Not this, not that, "neti, neti," disclaimer, asserting that all limitations are automatically to be rejected. For example, when asserting the positive characteristic of Personality, the theist will necessarily, if not reject, at least temporarily ignore, the possible characteristic of the Ultimate as Energy, Force, etc. The theist might then hurry to assert: Of course, all the positive characteristics of Energy, Force, etc., are also to be attributed to God. But this task goes on endlessly, or as Abe might say, with "boundless Openness." This the theist would gladly grant, but would want to add that this "boundless Openness," far from eliminating or negating the positive affirmations of Personality, Energy, etc., in fact gives them a boundless depth, dynamism, Openness—with which perhaps Masao Abe and much of Buddhism might also agree, and perhaps Taoism as well with its notion of "dynamic vacuity," kung ling.[15]

It should also be noted that how one describes Ultimate Reality is, among other things, dependent upon not only one's philosophical thought categories, but also upon one's culture more generally. What is thought to be of greatest value in a culture will be attributed to Ultimate Reality; the fact that Ultimate Reality is so described will, of course, in turn dialectically reinforce that value in the culture.

For example, when females were thought to be the sole source of life, and hence, power, divinities were described in female terms—which in fact is how divinities first turn up in human cultures—but when it was discovered that males also played a role in producing new life, male divinities came into existence. As cultures became patriarchal, it became less and less acceptable to refer to the divinity as female. Hence, for example, God became almost exclusively a male, father God in the Semitic traditions; it would have seemed denigrating and blasphemous to refer to God in female terms, because woman was of lesser value in the culture.[16]

So, it was also for a long time in Western culture concerning the notions of "being," "substance," "stability," and the like. These were high values in the culture, so naturally they were attributed to the Ultimate Reality. But now in the West immutability, substance, status quo, etc., are increasingly less exclusively valued as compared with change, relationality, evolution. Hence, earlier in the West where it would have been difficult to speak of Ultimate Reality as being in constant change, in complete relationship, etc., for it would have seemed to be saying that the Ultimate Reality was less than ultimate—with the recent cultural shift, to speak thus seems to be more and more appropriate. Consequently, a Methodist theologian, for example, could publish an article entitled, "Can God Be Change Itself?" and conclude in the affirmative, insisting that this was more in keeping with the original genius of the Hebrew God, whose very name, Yahweh, means "I will be who I will be"—always changing.[17]

But what about the apparently opposite trend in the modern Judeo-Christian tradition, namely, the emphasis not on the Emptiness of Ultimate Reality, of God, but on God's passion, commitment, involvement, in history, and particularly on the side of the oppressed—the talk of God as the "God of the Oppressed"? This tradition grew out of the line of the Hebrew prophets, continued in Judeo-Christian history, and was expanded in the nineteenth century as the Western awareness of the influence in human life of social structures grew, and that religion had to be concerned about changing them for the better if the individuals were to be changed for the better. This led in the last hundred years to, e.g., the Jewish passion for social justice, the Jüdischer Bund, Christian Socialism, the Social Gospel, and the several contemporary "liberation" theologies. One Christian answer has been that,

> Liberation theologies can themselves learn from Buddhism that the "God of the Oppressed" to whom they point is also a "God who is empty." ... in a Buddhist sense, referring to that absence of self subsistence and, hence, that radical relationality of which all beings are exemplifications. To say that God is "empty" is to say that God, too, is relational. It is to affirm (1) that the efficacy of God's action in the world depends partly on worldly response, and (2) that the world's sufferings are God's own.[18]

e) Imago Dei and Anatta

Gautama's understanding of authentic human life is expressed in his teaching of Anatta, discussed briefly above. Jesus's (or, as he was known in his lifetime, Yeshua's) understanding can be expressed in the teaching of the human being as the Image of God, Imago Dei, stemming from the first book of the Hebrew Bible. In its beginning the Bible tells of one God who is the source of all reality through creation. The crowning point of creation was humankind, who was made in God's image, that is, someone who could know and could freely decide, could love. Modern critics of religion would say that instead of homo being an Imago Dei, Deus is really an Imago Hominis—to which the modern theistic adherent of religion would respond that both are doubtless true in different but analogous ways.

In this tradition everything that exists is good simply because it has being, and this being springs from God, who is all good. Then whence evil—for to the Hebrews, as to everyone else, it was obvious that there was evil in the world, indeed, in every human being? Their answer was that human beings themselves are the source of evil, for by their free will they can refuse to choose the good, and their choice then is called evil. This understanding is embedded in the story of the "Fall" at the beginning of the book of Genesis: Because humanity did not follow the right order of their nature, their "self," as created by God, in God's image, it became "disordered" in its relationship to its own self and its creator, and hence in turn to all the rest of creation. Here was the first "domino theory."

Though the way to live an authentic human life is to live according to one's authentic "self," one's Imago Dei, perceiving that true self, that Imago Dei, became difficult after the "Fall" and so, according to the Hebrews, God arranged for special help to be made available, at least to a "Chosen People," the Hebrews, who in turn were to be "a light unto the nations." This special help were God's Instructions, God's Torah, on how to live a true human life, one in accordance with one's true self, the Imago Dei.

Thus, the Hebrew religion was basically optimistic, for the source of all reality was the one God, who was goodness itself, and God's creation was, as it says in Genesis, "good," Tov, and in the end even "very good," Mod Tov. But it also took account of the presence of evil in humans and prescribed its elimination by the human returning to its original authentic self, the Imago Dei, the clear path to which was indicated by God's Torah. And the heart of the Torah was justice and love, or even simply love, for, as Pope Paul VI said, "justice is love's minimum."[19]

The summary of the Torah was the two-fold commandment of love of God and love of neighbor, and the former could be carried out really through the fulfillment of the latter, the love of neighbor. Who, then, is the neighbor who is to be loved? The Hebrew prophets appeared in the history of the Hebrew people to make it abundantly clear that what God desired was not "burnt offerings" but rather a just life, and more, which meant not only treating everybody fairly, but preeminently loving the oppressed, the powerless, of society—and they specifically spoke of the poor, the widow, the orphan, the most powerless of society. Every human being, even the least in society, was an Imago Dei, and was to be treated as such.

f) Yeshua and Gautama: "Action-Oriented," Soteriocentric

Yeshua, from a theist, Jewish culture, was—like Gautama—from a non-theist, Indian culture, oriented toward action, concerned not with speculation but with the "cure of souls," with the full health, or Salus, of humanity. In this concern he drew from his Hebraic, Judaic roots.

Around 167 BCE, the Pharisees, who have had such unwarrantedly bad press in the Christian tradition, appeared on the scene. Among other things, they showed the "way" (Halachah in Hebrew) to lead a just, Jewishly human life, by laboring to make concrete the more general obligations found in the "written Torah," the Bible, and eventually their specifying commentary came to be understood as the "oral Torah." In all these reflections, for the Pharisees, as for Jews in general, the big question was not, "What must I think?" as it was for the Greeks and later also too much so for most Christians, but rather "What must I do?"

The Pharisees, of course, were not the only Jews at the beginning of the Common Era who laid claim to have the right teaching on how to live an authentic human, Jewish, life. There were others, and among those "others" was the Galilean Jew Yeshua of Nazareth, who in many ways was close to the Pharisees, but also critical of them. Yeshua of course was a Jew, religiously as well as ethnically. He studied the Jewish Scriptures, carefully kept the Torah, or "Law," indeed declared that he "had not come to abolish the Law but to carry it out" (plerosai, literally, to "implement"—see Matt. 5:17). Like the Pharisees, Yeshua also specified the general great two-fold commandment of love of God and neighbor; all his teaching and all his stories were aimed at making God's instructions, God's Torah, concrete. And like the other prophets—his followers also called him a prophet—he epitomized the love of neighbor in reaching out to the powerless: When asked, Who is leading an authentic human life, who will "enter into the kingdom of heaven"? he answered, those who give drink to the thirsty, food to the hungry, clothing to the naked (cf. Matt 25:35–36). For Yeshua also then, because he was a good Jew, the big question was not, "What must I think?" but "What must I do?"—not unlike Gautama's soteriocentric approach.

This then, in brief, was the "Good News," the "God-spel," Yeshua taught, that the Reign of God was near, indeed, "within you" (entos hymon—an interior and interrelational reality), and that letting "God reign" in their lives would lead them to joy now (again, like Gautama's focus on the "now"), and "in the world to come." Thus, the first followers of Yeshua, who of course were all Jews, found in him a special "way" (Halachah) to "salvation" (the term comes from the Latin Salus, meaning primarily a full, healthful, whole, and therefore [w]holy, life, not being "saved" by something or someone from the outside) by what he "thought, taught and wrought."

g) The Christ—The Buddha

The development of the meaning of Yeshua the Christ obviously provides many points of fruitful dialogue with Buddhism. Yeshua clearly was an extraordinary charismatic healer, teacher and prophet. But at least some of his first followers saw something else very special, very Jewish, in him; they saw him as the Messiah (Christos in Greek), the Anointed One, who, as promised in the Scriptures, would among other things free Judea from the hated Roman military occupation. But he did not. Rather, the Romans crucified him. At first Yeshua's followers were crushed. Two of them were reported to have said, "But we had hoped that he would be the one to redeem Israel" (Luke 24:21). But the power of Yeshua was too great for it all to run out through the cracks of the rock of Golgotha. For his followers, Yeshua rose bodily from the dead and further empowered them to go forth to preach his "Good News."

But what about the messianic claims of Yeshua's followers for him? He did not become the new political king of Israel. They, or at least some of them, did not drop the messianic claims, they simply transformed, spiritualized, the understanding of Messiah. However, as the "Way" of Yeshua moved from the Jewish to the Greek world, the Greek term Christ grew in usage and importance, and in a way that it became fused with another Jewish title given to Yeshua, namely, "son of God." The latter was a term used to refer to kings and holy men, obviously meant in a metaphorical way. In that Greek "field of force," as Yagi might put it, however, the metaphorical title "son of God" moved in a few centuries to the ontological title "God the Son," as reflected in the trinitarian formula of the Council of Nicaea (325 CE).

Many modern critical-thinking Christians, being aware of what occurred in the paradigm shift from the Jewish metaphorical thought world to the Greek substance-ontological thought world, ask themselves what the intended meaning was at the beginning of the process. One way some have of putting it is that the followers of Yeshua saw in him a transparency of the divine. He appeared to them to be so radically open to all being, including the Root of being, that he was completely filled with Being. Thus, he was a human meeting point of the human and the divine, an enfleshment, incarnation, of the divine, as all humans ought to be, and in principle can be—as Yeshua himself urged: "Be you perfect as my heavenly Father!" Thus, some modern Christians see this original Jewish perception of Yeshua as more "ortho-dox," "right-teaching," than some of the later Greek ontological/substance formulas.[20]

In this way Yeshua becomes for Christians a model of how to live an authentic human life. In him they meet Ultimate Reality, the divine, so that in a preeminent way he is for them the door to the divine, to be sure, not the only possible point of entree, but for them the one that informs all others, just as they see that Gautama does for the Buddhists, Mohammed for the Muslims, etc.

At the same time, it is also clear from the New Testament, especially from the Pauline writings and John's Gospel, that there was a tendency early in the history of the followers of Yeshua to become "Christocentric" rather than "Theocentric," that is, a tendency to "foreshorten" the follower's gaze from where or whom the mediator was pointing to (Theos) to the mediator himself (Christos). This did not mean that Paul and John forgot about God and concentrated solely on Christ. It does mean, however, that in their writings there is a great emphasis on getting to God through Christ, whereas in the Synoptic Gospels, which mainly portray Yeshua's teaching and actions (complicated, to be sure, by being seen through the lenses of the early faith communities) the strong stress is on God.

Moreover, it is important to note that Paul overwhelmingly talks about, not Yeshua, not Jesus, but about Christ, Jesus Christ, Christ Jesus. Most often Christ for Paul was not a concrete human person, but much more a spiritual "force" or "life," so that he could write things like, "I live now not I, but Christ lives in me." This notion of a "spiritual life" entering into one's own interior life fit quite well with the Semitic way of understanding and speaking of the world (as Seiichi Yagi also so fruitfully probed and compared with Buddhist thought), but it was all too liable to be "ontologized," understood as a "substance" in the Greek thinking world of the Roman Empire. This unfortunately did happen much too extensively. And when the "mind of Christ" was thus ontologized, the notion of salvation also tended to be understood as something coming from the outside, as if one were "saved" by Christ as by a sort of cosmic lifeguard, rather than be understood in its original meaning of being healthy, whole, (w)holy. Salvation came solely by "Other-Power," Tariki as it is expressed in Japanese Buddhist language, and not at all by "Self-Power," Jiriki.

Again, the question arises, as with substance thinking/relational thinking: Must one make a choice? Again, I believe the answer is yes and no. The answer is yes, one must choose Other-Power for if one wants to be a Christian, that means fundamentally that the Jew Yeshua of Nazareth is the key to the meaning of life and how to live it. How this Yeshua comes to inhere in one's life, of course, is a complex process, but it is obvious that he must in a variety of ways be "spiritualized" so he can be "interiorized" in another person's interior life, and consequent external behavior. Early in the history of the followers of Yeshua a major way that "interiorizing" was named was with the term Christ.

Hence, the answer is also no, a choice should not be made between Other-Power and Self-Power, for a Christian should build his Christian life on the foundation of Yeshua, on what he "thought, taught and wrought," as a model, and, having thus been energized, strive (Self-Power) to live accordingly—and at the same time understand and refer to that interiorized energy as Christ (Other-Power), as Paul did, for example. It is a matter of appropriate balance, but, of course, what constitutes a proper balance in one individual and one culture and one time and one place, may not be precisely the same in others. Our human reality is plural; hence, our means of Salus must correspondingly match it.

As already noted, one similarity between Buddhism and Christianity lies in the fact that both take their names not from the proper names of their founders, Gautama and Yeshua, but from two of their titles, Buddha, The Enlightened One, and Christ, The Anointed One. At the same time there is a contrast in that the title "The Enlightened One" tells us something about what happened to Gautama and also about the goal of his followers, whereas "The Anointed One" says something about whence Yeshua came, but nothing about the goal of his followers.

A much more striking and revealing similarity that is somehow embedded in the use of the titles for naming the religions is the divinizing move in an ontological sense that occurred in both. As already noted, in Christianity there very early developed a shift from the religion of Yeshua to the religion about Christ, from the human Yeshua to the divine Christ. A similar development took place in Buddhism, from the religion of the human Gautama to the religion about a quasi-divinized Buddha. Of course, the latter took place mainly only in Mahayana Buddhism, although on the popular level something like it also occurs widely in Hinayana, or Theravada, lands. On the other hand, the divinization move, in an ontological sense, pervaded almost all Christianity until late modern times.

An extended irenic dialogue in this area will doubtless shed a great deal of light on the "development of dogma" that has taken place, on both sides, on where it has been true to the initiating principles and founders, and on where it has wandered into blind alleys. It will also enable a "return to sources," which is vital in every renewal effort in all religions and institutions, to take place with more equanimity and balance, in tandem with the growth, adaptation and creativity that is likewise necessary in every religion and institution.

h) Prophet—Monk

In a number of ways, the "founders" of Buddhism and Christianity, Siddhartha Gautama and Yeshua of Nazareth, were quite similar: They were, for example, both men, both advocates of peaceful, non-violence means—in contrast, for instance, to Mohammed—both teachers, both peripatetics, both leaders of a band of followers. However, in a number of other ways they were quite different: Gautama, for example, apparently came from a rich family, Yeshua from a relatively poor one; Gautama lived to old age, Yeshua barely reached maturity; Gautama died from natural causes, Yeshua was ignominiously executed.

All these and other similarities and contrasts, besides the ones already discussed, merit study and reflection, but here I would like to lift up one particular contrast which has had a very large influence on the differing developments of Buddhism and Christianity, namely, Yeshua the prophet and Gautama the monk.

Yeshua stood very much in the Hebrew tradition of prophets, God's "spokespersons" (from pro-phetes in Greek, to "speak for" another) who in God's name challenged others to cease wrongdoing, especially injustice against the oppressed in society. Consequently, Yeshua's stress was on the proper ethical behavior toward other persons, especially the weak, and on the insistence that this was the major way to love God, to live an authentic human life. His followers were not understood as simply learners, but also as subsequent teachers, as "sub-prophets." Many were even called "those who are sent," aposteloi, who were to bear his "good news," Godspel, of the Reign of God.

On the other hand, Gautama did not understand himself as anything like a spokesperson of God, a prophet. He understood himself as a teacher who wanted to share his discovery, his insight, with others. However, his stress was on each person's own inner self, and only secondarily on interpersonal behavior. His followers did not simply go out as "ones sent," but formed an ongoing, a permanent, community of monks, the Sangha.

One must immediately utter a cautionary word, however, against absolutizing this contrast, for Yeshua also was concerned about the inner self—more about that below—and Gautama likewise taught a whole range of interpersonal ethics. Further, the followers of Yeshua did eventually form an ongoing community, the Ekklesia, the Church. Of course, the Sangha, an inner circle of monks (or to a much lesser extent, nuns) is quite different from the all-embracing Ekklesia. But then, Christianity also developed an inner circle of clergy and monks and nuns, and also Buddhism developed a close relationship between the lay community and the monks. Nevertheless, one can speak of major and minor stresses in each community, and in this area the two traditions seem to relate with each other not in "parallel" fashion, but "diagonal": the major stress in one is a minor stress in the other, and vice versa.

Clearly dialogue here will assist each side to see in the mirror of its partner its own strengths and corresponding weaknesses better, so that a creative balance—which will always be shifting with the shifting times and cultures—can be struck. One part of that dialogue, that among monks from both sides, and much less among nuns, has, as indicated above, begun. The dialogic concern for the wider community has not yet even been awakened—but it very much needs to be.

i) Faith Works: Tariki, Jiriki

Buddhists and Christians likewise have much to learn about themselves as well as each other in the great debate over whether one lives a worthwhile life ultimately by Self-Power or by Other-Power.

For Christians this debate is reflected already in the pages of the New Testament. There in the Letter of Paul to the Romans is found the one slogan, that one is "saved" by faith, by trust in Christ; also in the New Testament, in the Letter of James, is the other slogan, that faith without works is dead. In fact, there is not a contradiction in this matter in the New Testament writings, but there came to be one in the Christian interpretation given to those writings, especially by Augustine (pro-faith) in the West in his campaign against that much-maligned Irish

Christian, Pelagius (meaning "sea," Morgan in Irish), who stressed free will, Self-Power.

The debate erupted in all its fury in the sixteenth-century Protestant Reformation; it continued thereafter within the Catholic Church in the form of a struggle over grace and free-will, Thomism and Molinism, and in various branches of Protestantism, as in the Reformed Christian struggle between predestinationist Calvinism and free-will oriented Arminianism. It goes on in a number of ways to today, as for example in the contest between conservative Barthianism and Liberal Protestant Theology.

The same split occurs within Buddhism in a way already in the major division between Hinayana (only a few can attain nirvana) and Mahayana (many can attain nirvana) Buddhism. But the contrast is most visible in the two opposite forms of Buddhism which sprang up in China and were each promoted even more fully in Japan, namely, Pure Land Buddhism and Zen Buddhism. The former so thoroughly promotes faith in the grace of Amida Buddha that even Karl Barth affirmed that it could become almost acceptable to him, except that it was Amida Buddha instead of Christ that was the object of the trusting faith.[21] The latter, Zen Buddhism, of course emphasizes each individual's concentrating, either through reflection on Koans and the like or through sitting meditation, Zazen, until Enlightenment, Satori is achieved. The former stresses faith, Other-Power, Tariki, and the latter, works, Self-Power, Jiriki.

Again, careful, extended Buddhist-Christian dialogue in this area would greatly enlighten each partner about their own major dichotomy by seeing the same in the tradition of the partner, providing thereby the needed distance to be able to judge one's own division with greater perceptivity and calm. This would also lead to a greater sympathetic understanding of the partner's various forms of religiousness, particularly concerning Self-Power and Other-Power and how the two might be brought into creative polar tension rather than destructive divisiveness—"at home and abroad."

j) Creed—Code—Cult

Both Buddhism and Christianity understand themselves not as something just of the head or the hand or the heart, but as an entire way of life—in New Testament Greek the term used was Hodos and in Pali, Magga (most other religions also speak centrally of the "way": Judaism, Halacha; Islam, Shar'ia; Hinduism, Marga; Taoism and Confucianism, Tao; Shintoism, To). All three elements are of course present in both traditions: creed, code of behavior and cult (which, plus community-structure, make up the four c's of all religions and ideologies—the latter differing from the former in that they are not built on the understanding that Ultimate Reality is somehow transcendent, as the former are), but the mix will vary tremendously in each tradition depending on a variety of things, such as the various cultures in question, or whether one is dealing with popular-level or reflective religion.

It will be extremely enlightening for each partner to learn just how extraordinarily advanced the other has been in each of the categories. For example, it will doubtless at first be surprising to Christians to learn how penetrating a theological and philosophical set of systems have been developed in Buddhism, which quite thoroughly parallel their own theological and philosophical developments. The same will be true in the areas of ethics and cult. Even when they traveled abroad in the past, Christians have nevertheless often been quite insular in thinking that they alone had developed any proper ethical systems; an open extended dialogue will go a long way toward curing them of that isolationism.

Of course, East Asia has their own brand of triumphalism. China did not describe itself as the Chungguo, the "Central Kingdom," out of a sense of dialogue or egalitarianism. For a very long time the Chinese had a difficult time imagining that something worthwhile could come from outside of China. The Japanese in many ways still are no different today.

Nevertheless, there are new thoughts under the sun that have developed in Western culture, though not from Christianity directly. I am speaking not only of the fantastic advances in physical science and technology, but also of the new insights and entire ways of thinking in modern Western philosophical thought, the invention of the social sciences, and the creation of new social and economic structures, all of which are fast becoming the common good of the global modern world.

Within each of our religious communities these advanced techniques of thinking and living must be brought to bear on each of the areas of our own religion to probe, purge and promote it. But that constant task of renewal, of Aggiornamento, needs to be carried out not only alone but also in dialogic concert with persons from other religions, and in this case with Christians and Buddhists. Once again, in this dialogue each partner will learn things about themselves that would not be possible alone, and of course in this kind of irenic, self-critical encounter the similarities and differences of the partner will also be seen in a much more sympathetic light, conducing not only to a peaceful co-existence, but even a pro-existence.

k) Ethics: Individual—Social

The development of a code of ethics is at the very heart of all religions, and these codes always have both an individual and a social dimension. When a religion comes to dominate a culture and a state, its ethic tends to be incorporated into the customs and laws of that culture and state. This is obviously true, for example, for Judaism in Israel and Islam in many countries yet today. It was also true of Christianity in what was known as Christendom, and likewise of Buddhism at various times and places, as for example, in India under Ashoka, Emperor from 273 to 232 BCE.

However, these almost all occurred in what might be sociologically called "traditional" societies, ones in which there was a high degree of union of "church" and state. However, in the modern world, union of church and state is becoming less and less tenable (despite literally "reactionary" efforts in the Muslim world, which are painful—but I predict, passing—efforts at holding onto the past). This is not only because more and more countries and cultures are becoming religiously pluralistic under the impact of modern communications and travel, but also because with the spread of education and freedom, a truly free choice in religious matters is increasingly seen as authentically human and truly religious.

With the separation of church and state and the increase of freedom, first of all in Christendom, the religious social ethical dimension became increasingly a matter of the free choice of the individual, either singly or in groups. Then to the observer, individual ethics appeared to loom newly large in people's religious consciousness. In fact, however, it had always predominated, for in the past the masses really had no choice in matters of social justice; those matters were decided at the macro levels. However, with separation of church and state the true involvement, or rather, mostly non-involvement, of the masses of religious people in social justice issues beyond the immediately ameliorative became clear. As this occurred through the nineteenth and twentieth centuries, more and more committed Christians, and Jews, developed a strong involvement in theory and practice in social justice out of specifically Christian and Jewish motivations. Here the Hebrew prophetic tradition stood the proponents of the "Social Gospel," "Liberation Theology," Korean "Minjung Theology," and the like, in good stead.

In contrast, Eastern religions appeared to be almost solely committed to an individualistic ethic. However, religions of the East, and in particular Buddhism, have always considered virtues like compassion essential, and that has doubtless had an ameliorative effect on much human misery. Yet, the religions of the East probably even more than the Semitic religions have often been closer to being what Marx called "the opium of the people," an "escape" or consolation in this vale of tears which must be endured rather than changed. In any case, now in the East, as already earlier in the West, individual compassion and charity have increasingly been found inadequate to cope with the rising tide of modern social change; some of the Eastern religions, therefore, have recently also begun to see social justice and just structural social change as religious responsibilities.

In Thailand, for example, where one might least expect it, there are a number of efforts at engagement in social justice out of specifically Buddhist motivations. For example, in Bangkok Dr. Sulak Sivaraksa, a Theravada Buddhist layman, is extremely active in organizing a wide range of social action projects arising out of his Buddhist commitment.[22]

One of his spiritual mentors and one of the most important and influential Buddhist thinkers in Thailand for the past thirty years is the monk Buddhadasa, who has done a massive job in making the Buddhist scriptures available and applicable to contemporary Thai life. In the area of social ethics he promotes what he calls "Dhammic Socialism," a socialism based on the Buddhist Dhamma, or teaching[23], which he understands to be a middle ground between communism, "which does not sufficiently respect individual differences," and what he calls liberal democracy's "excessive individualism."[24] "In a dhammic socialistic society … the wealthy would be motivated to distribute their wealth as a result of the ideals of generosity and loving kindness instilled by religion and morality rather than being forced by the state."[25]

Phra Rajavaramuni is also a very important and influential thinker and activist in social justice issues qua Buddhist in Thailand.[26] He takes a rather startlingly positive attitude toward desire, productivity, individual freedom and democracy which does not fit the stereotype of Theravada Buddhism. For example, he distinguishes between a self-centered desire, tanha, and a positive kind of desire, chanda, which can be translated as the "desire for knowledge, an interest in knowledge and wanting to do, or taking an interest in doing what is correct and excellent. I believe that chanda is the axis of development [he is speaking here of economic and similar development], it is the thing which education must instill, and then we will not have the problem of desiring or not desiring, and we can stop talking about it altogether." He added: "We must make a distinction between a desire that is tanha and a desire that is dhammachanda."[27]

In Hong Kong, Buddhist monks who came from the mainland in 1949–50 after the Communist revolution have recently turned to social justice issues, partly, it is clear, as a result of their encounter with the social justice orientation of the Christian churches. Something similar is happening within traditional Buddhism in South Korea. More striking is Won Buddhism, founded in Korea in the second decade of this century. Won Buddhism works to combine the principles of Gautama Buddha with an affirmation of modern science and technology in working for the betterment of men and women, individually and collectively; hence, it is not surprising that the Won Buddhists also have a very strong commitment to interreligious dialogue.

The Catholic theologian and Buddhologist Aloysius Pieris notes that "The social dimension of Buddhist ethics is being reclaimed from oblivion and re-expressed as the Buddha's vision of a just political order for today, so that social justice is regarded at least as an inevitable by-product of Buddhist soteriology."[28] For example, some low caste Hindus sought freedom from their social lot in conversion to Buddhism and have produced a "Literature of the Oppressed." The following verse from a poem to Buddha is an example of this contemporary social liberation image of Buddha.

> I see you
> Speaking and walking
> Amongst the humble and the weak
> In the life-threatening darkness
> With torch in hand
> Going from hovel to hovel.
> Today you wrote a new page
> of the Tripitaka [early Buddhist scripture][29]

Pieris commented,

> This indeed is a new interpretation of the Buddha's soteriological role. The belief in his cosmic lordship is hermeneutically extended to the socio-political structures whose radical transformation is believed to be possible under the Buddha's soteriological influence. Undoubtedly, this is "a new page in the Tripitaka," as the poet declares.[30]

In this area of social justice, particular notice of the place of women in both Buddhism and Christianity should be taken. To begin with, it is clear that Yeshua took a radically egalitarian stand toward women, something which ran counter to his Semitic cultural context. As I have argued elsewhere, "Jesus Was a Feminist."[31] This positive attitude toward women obviously continued to a large extent during the early decades after the lifetime of Yeshua, as is evidenced in the recording of the large amount of pro-woman material in the four Gospels, and even the largely egalitarian attitude expressed in the authentic letters of Paul.[32] However, as the band of the followers of Yeshua moved from an apocalyptic expectation of an imminent end of the world as they knew it to a church structured to endure a long period of time, women were increasingly repressed, until very modern times when the women's movement in the West began to liberate women more and more in society in general and in the Christian churches as well.

The situation was somewhat different in Buddhism. Gautama apparently taught women as well as men, but there is a legend that he said that the Sangha would decline much sooner if women were allowed to become nuns than if they were not; nevertheless, at the urging of his disciple Ananda, Gautama did allow women to become nuns. Whether this legend has any historical basis is open to question not only because the written document comes into existence only after hundreds of years of oral tradition, but even more so because this oral tradition and written document come to us from the all-male monks, who might well have distorted it.[33]

In any case, women have had a checkered career in subsequent Buddhism, holding in general, as in Christianity, second-class status. In Buddhism, too, however, a sense of egalitarianism is beginning to assert itself and a Buddhist feminist movement is starting to develop,[34] though it lags far behind the religious feminist movement in Christianity. However, equal justice for women is a cause that will increasingly appear on the dialogue agenda between Buddhists and Christians, and can be only beneficial to both.

There is much that Christians and Buddhists can share in dialogue in this area of individual and social ethics, and perhaps even more important, there are many issues of social justice wherein Christians and Buddhists can cooperate for the good of all. Here dialogue in the "practical" sphere might well come to the fore.

In sum: Interreligious dialogue, and specifically Buddhist-Christian dialogue, is taking place with accelerating frequency on all different levels, concerning an increasing number of subjects and in many different places. There is obviously a growing amount of good will and a rapidly expanding body of shared information, which more and more makes a clarity of interpretation and translation of that information into commonly understood language and expression a high priority.

It is precisely in this situation that Seiichi Yagi is doing his preeminent work of theological interpretation and translation in a Christian-Buddhist dialogic context, preparing the way for the next century when, "Outstanding representatives of Zen Buddhism have read the gospel, and some of them believe that the great event of the 21st century will be the encounter and unity of Christianity and Buddhism."[35] As the founder in the early part of this century in Korea of the sect Won Buddhism, the Great Master Sotaesan said, "Enlightened men, however regard all religions as one family under one roof,"[36] and the Won Buddhist Steering Committee for United Religions more recently wrote:

> The basic, fundamental truth of all religions cannot but be one. In addition, even though each religion's means of education may be different, the goal being sought cannot but be one. … All religions urgently need to open their doors wide, assemble in one place and discuss, train and enact joint operations for the sake of mutual understanding and cooperation.[37]

Buddhism and Christianity in Japan

One of the places of the most creative encounters between Buddhism and Christianity is Japan, where the East meets the West. Japan is also the culture which has produced Seiichi Yagi and his creative dialogue between Buddhism and Christianity. Thus, if Yagi and his work are to be properly understood, they must be seen within the context of the development of Buddhism and Christianity in Japan. Let us look first at Buddhism and then Christianity in Japan.

Buddhism in Japan

Already in India, Gautama's homeland, Buddhism developed the Hinayana (small vehicle) and Mahayana (large vehicle) approaches, with the former stressing that only the few can hope to reach nirvana and the latter that the many can so hope. Both versions were exported to China. However, only the more practical, this-worldly Mahayana version of Buddhism had a chance of being accepted by the Chinese—some versions of "Hinayana" Buddhism also reached China, but died aborning. Mahayana Buddhism, however, was so successful in China that it became known as one of the three religions of China (Taoism and Confucianism being the other two). In fact, it became at times the "state" religion, reaching its apogee in the first half of the ninth century.

Chinese Buddhism, like Indian Buddhism, was also fertile in the development of various strands of Buddhism. Their major schools can perhaps be helpfully divided into two groups, those with a "catholic" or comprehensive orientation, namely: Tian-tai (in Japan, Tendai), Hua-yen (in Japan, Kegon) and the Esoteric school, Mi Tsung (in Japan, Shingon); and those with a "protestant" or selective perspective, namely: Ch'an (in Japan, Zen), Ching T'u Tsung or Pure Land (in Japan, Jodo-shu and Shin-shu)—

in Japan a third major "protestant" sect was formed that is uniquely Japanese, that is, Nichiren Buddhism.[38]

The three "catholic" sects in content were, very briefly, as follows: Tian-tai Buddhism was developed in the sixth century by Chi-i (538–597), who saw the culmination of Buddhist wisdom in the first-century Mahayana writing, the Lotus Sutra, which declared that all beings will be saved, and that finally "all is one, that all moments of existence inhere in a grain of sand, suggesting that all life is caught up in one moment of life"[39]—and the way to arrive at this truth was through meditation. Hua-yen Buddhism, very similar to Tian-tai, was brought to flower by Fa Tsang (643–712) and other monks, the major difference being that Fa Tsang thought the Hua-yen Sutra rather than the Lotus Sutra was the acme of Buddhist wisdom.

The two major "protestant" types of Buddhism grew up inside of Chinese Mahayana Buddhism during the same creative period, namely, the sixth century: Ch'an Buddhism (the Chinese transcription of the Sanskrit Dhyana, meaning meditation—in Japanese it is pronounced Zen); and Ching T'u Tsung, Pure Land Buddhism (from the Sanskrit Sukhavati, meaning a paradise this side of nirvana). Although they both had the general characteristics of Mahayana Buddhism, they were in some ways quite opposite to each other. Ch'an emphasized the attainment by means of meditation, stressing thereby Gautama's own teaching of each individual striving to attain nirvana—Self-Power, or Jiriki, as the Japanese put it. On the other hand, Pure Land Buddhism developed the legend of the Amitabha (Amida in Japanese) Buddha who took a vow not to enter nirvana until he had brought all human beings into the paradise of the Pure Land—and this can be accomplished simply by calling upon the name in trust of the Amitabha Buddha—Other-Power, or Tariki in Japanese.

From China Buddhism moved into Korea, where, as in China, it frequently absorbed many elements of Confucianism, and also local shamanism which was still strong—and is yet until today. From there Buddhism came to Japan in the middle of the sixth century. Although the Koreans themselves apparently did not completely understand this "new" religion, they obviously appreciated it very highly, partly because it came with recommendations from what they considered the best sources, China, and even far-away India.

In 552 the Korean king of Paekche sent gifts to the emperor of Japan, including Buddhist materials, saying: "This doctrine [Buddhism] is among all doctrines the most excellent. But it is hard to explain, and hard to comprehend. … [It] can … lead to a full appreciation of the highest wisdom. ... From distant India it has extended higher to the great Han [China] where there are none who do not receive it with reverence."[40]

a) The Nara and Heian Periods

After a relatively hesitant beginning in Japan, Buddhism was embraced by Prince Shotoku (574–622 CE), who became regent in 593 and proceeded to invite Buddhist monks from Korea and send students off to China. In just over a hundred years, in 710, a new capital was founded at Nara and was quickly heavily influenced by the Buddhist monasteries springing up all around. This influence became so stressful that in 794 still another new capital was established, at Heian-kyo (modern Kyoto), to get away from the ubiquitous monks.

It was early during this Heian period (794–1185) of Japanese history that two Japanese Buddhist sects that are still important today were founded. They both have Chinese counterparts from which they sprang. The one is Tendai (Tian-tai in Chinese), which was started by the monk Saicho, posthumously known as Dengyo Daishi (Daishi means great teacher—762–822). The second comes from the Chinese Esoteric or Mi Tsung school and in Japanese is known as Shingon (meaning "true word," taken from the alternative Chinese name for the school, Chen Yen, which has the same meaning); it was founded by Kukai, posthumously known as Kobo Daishi (773–835).

b) The Kamakura Period

The general situation in Japan so deteriorated during the latter part of the Heian period that civil war broke out, ending with the establishment of the shogunate capital in Kamakura, not far from present-day Tokyo. The emperor and the many Buddhist temples and monasteries remained in Heian while military, economic, and in general, governing, matters were handled in the name of the emperor by the shogun. This period turned out to be the most creative for Japanese Buddhism since not only was this when the three "protestant" sects were established in Japan, but in addition, they were launched by founders whose thought continues to have profound influence even until today.

c) Nichiren Buddhism

Nichiren Buddhism, which has no counterpart in China, is named after its founder Nichiren (1222–1282), who took that name for himself (literally "Sun Lotus"). Nichiren tried Pure Land and Zen Buddhism (discussed below) and found them wanting; he then went to a Tendai monastery and, like its founder Saicho, found the acme of wisdom in the Lotus Sutra. However, he was convinced that Tendai Buddhists had drifted away from their origins, and so he started on his prophetic way to call them and all Japan to embrace the Lotus Sutra without reservation.

Nichiren was a prophet in the most irascible, pugnacious sense. He denounced all other leaders in Buddhism, often in vitriolic language, as heretics who should be killed and whose traitorous brands of Buddhism should be suppressed. (One might wonder what Gautama Buddha would have thought of such a position so obviously at odds with his life and teaching being advocated under the name of Buddhism, but then one might also do the same for Jesus Christ and the preaching of the medieval Inquisition of precisely the same period.)

Nichiren stressed a kind of "millenarianism" which, following an ancient tradition, taught that for the first thousand years after the death of Gautama there would be Buddha's teaching, practice and the attainment of Enlightenment; during the second thousand years there would be Buddha's teaching and practice, but no attainment of Enlightenment; during the third period (called Mappo), which supposedly was just beginning at the time of Nichiren, there would be only the teaching of Buddha; and one could be saved during this period only by following the teaching of the Lotus Sutra, which Nichiren was sent to preach.

(This in many ways sounds much like the teaching of the spiritual Franciscan Jacopone da Todi of thirteenth-century Christian Europe who taught that there were three periods in the history of humanity: the age of the Father, to the birth of Jesus; the age of the Son, until the thirteenth century; the age of the Spirit, which was beginning during his lifetime—and he came to preach it!)

Moreover, Nichiren was convinced that this leading of the world to safety by the teaching of the Lotus Sutra was to be accomplished by Japan, which had become the center of the world (Hegel did something of the same, though much less violently, with Protestant Christianity and Germany). Further, Japan was to be led to fulfill its mission by following Nichiren; he vowed: "I will be the Pillar of Japan; I will be the Eyes of Japan; I will be the Great Vessel of Japan. Inviolable shall remain these oaths."[41]

It is not difficult to understand how Nichiren Buddhism has had a strong influence on Japanese patriotism and nationalism. In all the forms of Nichiren (because of its sectarian mentality it has tended to divide and re-divide constantly) there has always been a strong stress on the unity of the phenomenal world and the absolute, and that "salvation" is to be worked out in the everyday, and very much so in political and social activity in the here and now. This is true in varying degrees as well of the new religions that have come out of Nichiren, such as Sokka Gakkai, Reiyukai, and Rissho Kosei Kai. (It should be noted that the growth of new Japanese religions after World War II has been so phenomenal that at least one in three Japanese are participants in one of them—while in many instances also retaining their active membership in their more traditional religious communities.)

d) Pure Land Buddhism

Pure Land Buddhism in Japan had two major founders, Honen (1133–1212) and his disciple Shinran (1173–1262). While in the monastery, Honen learned to recite the prayer Namu Amida Butsu, "Praise to Amida Buddha," shortened to Nembutsu, which originally was meant to call up an image of Amida Buddha and his Pure Land as in meditation. Honen was not the first Japanese monk to thus call on Amida Buddha, but he committed himself so completely to its efficaciousness that he drew a huge following. He was so convinced of the corruptness of human nature (as a young lad he experienced the violence of the civil war—his father being killed by bandits when he was eight years old) that he felt humans could be saved only by an outside power (Tariki), namely, that of Amida Buddha, who had vowed to bring all those who call on his name with trust to the Pure Land at the end of their lives. It was largely this stress on potential universal salvation that brought him such popularity. He wrote:

> There shall be no distinction, no regard to male or female, good or bad, exalted or lowly; none shall fail to be in His Land of Purity after having called, with complete desire, on Amida. Just as a bulky boulder may pass over the sea, if loaded on a ship, and accomplish a voyage of myriads of leagues without sinking; so, we, though our sin be heavy as stone, are borne on the ship of Amida's primeval vow and cross to the other shore without sinking in the sea of repeated births and deaths.[42]

One of the results of Honen's radical position, and its popularity, was that at the age of seventy-four he was exiled for some four years; nevertheless, his following, called Jodo-shu (Pure Land School) flourished.

One of Honen's followers into exile was Shinran, who had joined a monastery at age eight, but found the monastic life difficult to follow, and hence was strongly attracted by Honen's teaching. He even went so far in his rejection of the efficaciousness of asceticism that he married (it is said that he did so upon the advice of Honen in order dramatically to show the valuelessness of "works") while continuing to be a monk. Shinran went even further in his view of the utter helplessness of humans and their complete dependence on the "good favor," the "grace" of Amida Buddha to be saved:

> Whether sage or fool, whether good or bad, we have simply to give up the idea of estimating our own qualities or of depending upon self. Though entangled in sin and depravity, even in living the life of the most despised outcast, we are embraced by the all-pervading light of grace; indefatigable faith in salvation itself is a manifestation of Buddha's act of embracing us into His grace, because nothing can impede the working of His grace.
>
> Nothing is required except to accept Amida without question. The Nembutsu is neither practice nor virtue to one who practices it. As it is not practiced through one's own will or power, it is no practice; as it is not virtue perfected by one's own will or power, it is no virtue. It solely arises from Other-Power [Tariki] and has nothing to do with Self-Power [Jiriki].[43]

Indeed, two of Luther's "mottos" are extraordinarily exemplified here: one is saved by faith alone, sola fide, and by grace alone, sola gratia. Of course, instead of Luther's only Christ, solus Christus, Shinran held fast to only Amida, sola Amida.

The followers of Shinran are referred to as members of Shin-shu, the Faith School. However, "As the closest of friends may have the most intense quarrels, so the two groups [Honen's Jodo-shu and Shinran's Shin-shu] have often been vigorous rivals. Nevertheless, cordial relations have generally prevailed."[44] They constitute the largest religious body in Japan, which already in the 1960s had over thirty-five million members.[45]

e) Zen Buddhism

The third major Buddhist tradition that flowered in the Kamakura period, like Pure Land Buddhism, also had two founding figures of major stature, who consequently gave birth to two major sects. They were Eisei (1141–1215), the founder of Rinzai Zen Buddhism, and Dogen (1200–1253), the founder of Soto Zen Buddhism (there are in fact over twenty different Zen Buddhist sects in Japan). Both went to China to study and there came into contact with different versions of Ch'an Buddhism, which they each brought back and developed in their own distinctive fashions.

Eisei immersed himself in the Lin-chi (the name of the Chinese founder, which was transmuted in Japanese into Rinzai) sect of Ch'an, which stressed attaining Enlightenment (Satori in Japanese) in a sudden flash, especially by meditating on non-rational puzzles, called Koans, and paradoxical dialogues, called Mondos.

Dogen studied far and wide in China, but only at the end of his stay did he attain Enlightenment, through a monk of the T'sao T'ung sect (which name was transmuted in Japanese into Soto) of Ch'an. Dogen mistrusted Koans and Mondos, and consequently concentrated on teaching that Zazen, sitting meditation, for long periods was the best path to Enlightenment, which most likely would come only in gradual fashion.

For Zen Buddhism in general, Enlightenment, Satori, is not something intellectual in a discursive, rational sense. Rather, it is something to be obtained by intuition, an immediate kind of cognitive experience. To be sure, it is something cognitive, but not in the everyday narrowly rational, analyzing manner of cognition, which is accomplished "mediately," by "running through," discursively, a number of steps to arrive at the concluding knowledge. Rather, the knowledge is arrived at immediately, by a direct union of the knower with the known.

This emphasis on unity is particularly strong in Dogen, who has been said to be "the greatest philosophic mind in Japanese history":

> Primary among the dualities of thought for Dogen was what he termed the distinction between original enlightenment and acquired enlightenment. The latter is the experience of satori or enlightenment which is sought by Zen Buddhists, while the former is the innate Buddha-nature, latent in all men and all things. These two are really one, declared Dogen characteristically. Thus, the achievement of enlightenment consists of the present realization of the original Buddha-nature.[46]

(We will find this distinction turning up below in the twentieth-century Christian thinkers Katsumi Takizawa and Seiichi Yagi.)

What comes through especially clearly in this quotation is the Zen stress on the this-worldliness of salvation, which in Buddhism takes the form of claiming that "Nirvana is samsara and samsara is nirvana." It is within this concrete life in the world (samsara) that humans are to find salvation (nirvana), not in escaping from this world by asceticism or looking toward the future (the Pure Land, heaven or the like). Rather, an authentic human life is to be lived fully now. Of course, in Zen great discipline is demanded so as to concentrate on finding one's true self (Zen's understanding of the doctrine of Anatta). Thus, Zen is fond of speaking of Ultimate Reality not as either personal or impersonal, but rather as transpersonal, that is, as not less-than-personal, but more-than-personal.

On the one hand it would also appear very obvious that Zen Buddhism emphasizes Self-Power, Jiriki—quite unlike Pure Land Buddhism, which stresses the utter necessity of Other-Power, Tariki. However, perhaps paradoxically, at the same time there is also in Zen Buddhism a sense of dependence: "While man must walk the path to enlightenment in his own strength, satori is not so much something men do as it is something which happens to them, and it does so in ways independent of human will or volition. Such, at least, is the experience that Zen Buddhists report."[47]

Although Zen Buddhism's membership is not as numerous as that of Pure Land Buddhism's, it nevertheless has had a massive influence on Japanese religious life and culture in general. It, along with Shintoism, was formative of the samurai culture which was so pervasive of Japanese culture since the Middle Ages; in fact, the whole of modern Japan flows from the post-1868 Meiji reforms which were accomplished by a small group of highly disciplined samurai. This Zen influence was seen not only in Zen swordsmanship, but also in the "softer" sides of life, as the tea ceremony, stylized Noh dramas, haiku poetry, flower arrangement, Zen gardens, and in general a reticent, inwardly-controlled behavior.

In many ways Buddhism in Japan, especially Zen and Nichiren and its many offshoots, but even to some extent Pure Land Buddhism, has moved 180 degrees from the Hinayana kind of Buddhism of India of 2,500 years ago. It has shifted from a focus on a rather elite, exclusive community of monks (and perhaps nuns) who alone had a chance to attain nirvana, to a totally inclusive community of monks, nuns and laity, including a largely married clergy (the monks, not the nuns—sexism is still culturally rampant in East Asia). Much of Buddhist life in Japan is centered on this life, nirvana in samsara, in many instances even entering actively—culturally, socially, politically—into secular life to reshape it.

It should also be noted that most Japanese will not be adherents of just one religion. The majority will actively retain substantial elements of the "big three," Shintoism, Confucianism and Buddhism, in various dimensions of their life, and at the same time the majority will live what to Westerners appears to be a quite "secular" life.

Christianity in Japan

By the fourth century, and even before, the religion of Yeshua had largely, though of course not entirely, become the religion about Christ. It was no longer simply Yeshua's "way"; it had become Christianity, the state religion of the mighty Roman Empire. Some form of Christianity also moved eastward from Israel into adjacent lands and by the fourth century reached India, but it had relatively little impact. One version of Christianity, Nestorianism, moved into China in the sixth century, but again had relatively little influence. In the fourteenth century Catholic Christianity came into the north of China, brought by Franciscans and supported by the Mongolian Emperor, but in less than a century it largely disappeared along with the Mongolian dynasty.

Then in the sixteenth century the great Catholic missionary movement paralleling European discovery voyages and colonization brought a Catholic version of Christianity to India and from there to Japan and Korea, and only later to China. Under the initial leadership of the Jesuit Francis Xavier Christianity made great strides in Japan, with many hundreds of thousands becoming Christian by the first third of the seventeenth century. But then its own success contributed to its downfall as the new rulers, the Tokugawa Shoguns, decided to close Japan off from outside influence, and Christianity was perceived as an outside religion. Hence, bloody persecution brought about many deaths and drove what few Christians remained underground without clergy or normal ways to sustain themselves.

In China developments were somewhat similar in that after a very difficult but brilliant beginning by the Jesuit Matteo Ricci, several hundreds of thousands of Chinese had become Christian by the end of the seventeenth century. But then out of theological myopia, and probably also a good deal of jealousy on the part of the Franciscans and Dominicans against the Jesuits, the Papacy took a number of restrictive and intolerant steps, the so-called "Chinese Rites Dispute," which put Christianity in such an unfavorable position that the number of Christians instead of continuing to grow, shrank to a small remnant.

Only in the nineteenth century did Protestant Christianity launch its missionary movement, largely paralleling, though with a certain time lag, the spread of the British Empire, coming into India, China, Korea and Japan, the latter two only in the last third of the nineteenth century, when those two countries were forcibly opened up to the West.

All this was initially done to "save the souls" of the "heathens," who, if not baptized, would go to hell. Nevertheless, despite huge efforts, Christianity has had relatively little success in East Asia, except in the Spanish-colonized Philippines, and in most recent times in southern Korea, where perhaps as much as 40 percent of the population has become Christian in the past few decades.

Only in 1859, in the wake of Commodore Perry's warships, could Catholic missionaries return to Japan after more than 200 years of exclusion; at the same time Protestant missionaries came to Japan for the first time. Despite the expenditure of great amounts of energy and sums of money, the number of Japanese who subsequently became Christian was small, a mere 1 percent of the population today. Probably the basic reason for this meager showing is symbolized by Perry's warships, that is, Christianity was perceived—and in fact largely comported itself as—a foreign import. Perhaps ironically, that same quality, its foreignness, its Westernness, at the same time provides it with an importance and influence disproportionate to its tiny numbers.

Part of this disproportionate influence comes from Christianity's significant educational establishment of high quality all the way through the university level, and part from its heavy commitment for the oppressed of society in Japan and elsewhere in Asia, led in a very visible way by the Catholic Church's "Commission for Justice and Peace,"[48] in which a quiet but major force both in Japan and elsewhere in Asia have been persons like Sister Filo Hirota (who, as of February, 1989, left to work in Nicaragua).

A description of Japanese Christian theology in general as being largely conservative and non-Japanese is in the main valid.[49] It is only in more recent times that deviations from this pattern have begun to appear, against great resistance.

Japanese Protestant theology has gone through three major phases since the re-introduction of Christianity into Japan a century and a half ago, largely paralleling cultural and theological developments in the West:

I. A purely Western theology was transmitted, which was to convert, but not to have any exchange with, things Japanese; this lasted till after World War I (there was one important exception to this in the Non-Church movement, started in the latter part of the nineteenth century by the well-known Protestant writer Kanzo Uchimura [1861-1930], which stressed individual faith and practice operating outside ecclesiastical institutions).[50]

II. Both Neo-Orthodoxy and the Social Gospel were stressed, the former represented especially in Tokutaro Takakura and the latter in Toyohiko Kagawa; this lasted until after World War II.

III. Liberal Protestant influences slowly came more to the fore, although conservative Barthian influences remained strong.

In this latter category, two theologians stand out after the war for attempting to bring liberal Protestant theology, mainly German in source, into contact with Japanese culture, without, however entirely rejecting Karl Barth,[51] namely Masatoshi Doi and Masao Takenaka.

However, the four Protestant Japanese theologians who have been the most creative in indigenizing their Christian theology are: Kazoh Kitamori, Katsumi Takizawa, Seiichi Yagi (who will be mentioned separately below) and Sasagu Arai.

Sasagu Arai has developed a kind of Japanese Liberation Theology, taking a sociological approach to both Jesus and contemporary Japan. He sees Jesus's life as one of sacrifice for the oppressed and the state of Jesus's time and contemporary Japan as an instrument of alienation, for it oppresses the lower classes; hence, Christians must return to Jesus to experience the same liberation that he brought through his cross.

The other three theologians all share a reaching out to other Japanese religions. Kazoh Kitamori was the earliest and most internationally known. His famous Theology of the Pain of God[52] was first published in 1946 and subsequently translated into English, German, Spanish, and Italian. His theology was born out of the pain and suffering of the war and is a kind of theology of the cross. In it he also draws upon the theme of suffering often occurring in Japanese Buddhism and classical drama, and is heavily influenced by the philosopher Hajime Tanabe's effort to find a Buddhist synthesis of opposites. He understands human pain to penetrate to the interior of God, and thus his notion of God is at least partially like that of process theology mentioned above. He is critical of Barth for making God too "completely other" and liberal Protestant theology for focusing too exclusively on God's love. His theological position, however, tends to place him largely outside Japanese Christian theology, of which fact he is aware.

Katsumi Takizawa published his pioneer work on Buddhism and Christianity[53] in 1964, in which he spoke of the "Immanuel Principle." By that he meant that every human has within her or him the immediate presence of God; this is the primary contact with God or Ultimate Reality. When, however, a person becomes aware of this primary reality, a second level of contact occurs, which he calls the secondary contact. Although the secondary contact occurs in a radical way with persons like Yeshua and Gautama, it is in principle available to all, and in fact is the goal of all, as is also urged in the teaching of both Yeshua and Gautama. (This distinction is very much like that of Dogen's described above, and is utilized by Seiichi Yagi in this volume and elsewhere.)

Japanese Catholic theology also largely paralleled the conservative path of Japanese Protestant theology in the beginning. After 1859 two factors worked strongly for conservatism. One was the fact that at that time Pius IX, the author of the reactionary "Syllabus of Errors" and the initiator of Vatican I with its declaration of papal infallibility, was on the papal throne. A second was that many of the underground Japanese Christians who had somehow survived the 200-year long Tokugawa persecution joined the Japanese Catholic Church, bringing their backward-looking Renaissance/Baroque style Catholicism with them.

The conservative, essentially Neo-Thomist approach continued unabated until Vatican II (1962–65), when dialogue with the world and with other religions and ideologies was strongly urged. With this new Copernican turn Western Catholic theologians living and working in Japan, e.g., Enomiya Lasalle, Heinrich Dumoulin and William Johnston, and Japanese Catholic theologians, e.g., Kakichi Kadowaki, Shigeto Oshida and Ichiro Okumura, began to develop indigenous Japanese elements in their theology, particularly through dialogue with Buddhism and also Shintoism.[54] Yōji Inoue also is attempting to work out a Christian theology that will spring from two sources, the Bible and Japanese culture.[55]

In addition, there is also the literary presentation of the experience of Christ by several Protestant as well as Catholic novelists.[56] "As is well known, the success of their books on Jesus Christ is a nationwide phenomenon. These novelists reach many non-Christians through their publications."[57] Doubtless the most important and widely read is the internationally known Catholic novelist Shusaku Endo.

Nevertheless, it is the judgment of one observer that what has been produced until now "can be considered the beginnings of Catholic theological reflection along Japanese lines. … But the first real Japanese theologians have yet to break through."[58]

Seiichi Yagi's Theology

Dialogue, Relationality, Integration

Seiichi Yagi is one of a several contemporary Japanese Christian theologians who use dialogue as a fundamental method to get at the heart of what it means to be an authentic human being, an authentic Christian. True to the essence of dialogue, he searches for new insight, new knowledge, not just for the sake of cerebration, but "to the end of constructive change both of ourselves and of the traditions to which we belong."[59]

Related to dialogue, Yagi wrote at length about a Japanese Buddhist term, which has become very important in his own thinking, Jiji-muge; it fundamentally refers to the interrelatedness, the interpenetration of all phenomena. However, "the term points, too, to dialogue with others at a depth where interpenetration becomes possible—where even, as Yagi says, the other becomes part of myself."[60] This image is very reminiscent of another image, developed quite independently by the American Jewish Jungian psychologist Ira Progoff, who speaks of individuals going down deep into the well of their inner selves until they reach an underground river which flows interconnectedly between individuals.[61]

We are here, in fact, at the center of Yagi's theology, which might be summed up in two words, relationality and integration. As is stressed in process philosophy—although that does not seem to have been the source and inspiration of Yagi's insight—beings do not exist in isolation from each other, but rather in radical relatedness to each other; relationality is constitutive of their very being. For humans, Thomas Aquinas put the matter very succinctly: "*Persona est relatio.*"[62] For Seiichi Yagi, "To perceive intuitively—to experience—this fact is a central element of the reality of religious salvation."[63]

Thinking, experiencing, living according to this radical relatedness of all reality is, according to Yagi, to live not splintered and divided, but integrated lives, lives within the womb of the oneness, which nevertheless embraces the manyness, of all reality. Yagi affirms that the manyness within the oneness of reality—and conversely—is affirmed by perceiving all beings not as separate entities, but as poles which are mutually dependent. For example, there can be no north pole without a south pole; the one is unthinkable without the other. Thus, "the integration of persons in polar (mutually interdependent, mutually respectful) relationship is the true end of human life, indeed of all life."[64]

One source and inspiration of this relational, integrative thinking of Yagi's is the Mahayana Buddhist concept of *pratītyasamutpāda*, dependent co-origination, the doctrine of the interrelatedness of all reality and, negatively expressed, the rejection of separate substance thinking, briefly discussed above. The second source and inspiration is the central Judeo-Christian notion of love. By love, "no man is an island," but reaches out from within to all being, and ultimately to the Root and Source of all being, and in turn is sustained and loved by that Source, "in whom we move, live and have our being," as Paul once quoted from a Greek poet. Thus, "both Christianity and Buddhism understand reality in the frame of integration."[65]

Ultimate Reality

Yagi does not see Christianity set over against Buddhism by the former's insistence on the Transcendent and the latter's denial or lack of it. Rather, he sees the Transcendent present in Buddhism from its beginning and in all of its major historical forms. For him the Buddhist notion of emptiness, sunyata, is, as described above, not a mere negative absence of being, but rather a fullness of potentiality, and the theist understanding of God is that of the Ground of Being, the infinite Source—two notions which by no means are totally alien to each other.

For Yagi both Christianity and Buddhism aim to lead its followers from an ego-centered existence to, as John Hick puts it, a "Reality-centered" existence.[66] Yagi designates this distinction in terminology he developed, namely, the movement from operating through the "mere Ego" to the "Self." Here, among other things, he draws on Yeshua's and Christianity's language of giving up one's life in order to gain it anew at a higher level, and Gautama's and Buddhism's language about cutting through all the false selves to the "original self," which is at times termed the No-Self, Anatta, in order to emphasize the relationality, the "non-separate substance" character of the authentic self.

The Transcendent, Ultimate Reality, Yagi likes to describe with the modern physics term, a "field of force," which has something of the quality of the Pauline/Greek womb description, "in whom we live, move and have our being," and also something of the Tillichian "Ground of Being." But it also conveys the notion of an all-pervasive reality without at the same time destroying the individuality of each being within the field. Of course, this metaphor stresses only the non-personal quality of the Transcendent, of Ultimate Reality, but no single metaphor can completely describe anything, let alone Ultimate Reality. Nevertheless, this metaphor does help modern people grasp an aspect of Ultimate Reality in a manner that they can relate to.

Yagi also makes use of the Mahayana doctrine of the three bodies of Buddha, the trikaya, described briefly above with the Buddhist Masao Abe's interpretation of it. For Yagi too, the dharmakaya is the Ultimate Reality, sunyata, God. At the other end is the nirmanakaya, which is manifested in historical figures like Yeshua and Gautama. Thus far this is the same as Abe. But the middle body, sambhogakaya, instead of being manifested by the gods of individual religions, such as Yahweh, Allah, Shiva, is related by Yagi to the Amida (in Japanese; Amitabha in Sanskrit) of Pure Land Buddhism and the Christ of Christianity—not the historical Yeshua but the cosmic figure, the Logos incarnate, that is, as related to humans. Thus, this trinity, like Abe's, is also a kind of modalism of the Transcendent.

This modalist way of thinking also recommended itself to many ancient Christian thinkers when wrestling with the issue of the trinitarian God-language they felt they found in the Bible, but given the Greek separatist-substantialist thought categories they operated with, such an "obvious"—to the metaphorical thinking and speaking Jews who formulated the biblical language—solution as modalism was unacceptable, and so trinitarian modalism was condemned as a Christian heresy. Today, with an increase of more relational, process thought categories and a great increase in understanding of the biblical thought world and language, such modal ways of thinking and speaking again are coming to the fore.[67]

Moreover, as soon as it is perceived and accepted that modern modalism is cast in categories of the new paradigm of relational process thought, the charge of heresy will fall away. However, as with all major paradigm shifts, resistance by those in power who still live and think in the old paradigm (in this case, static, separatist-substantialist in character) will be tenacious. Thus, Yagi, among others, is the object of this resistance.

Paul and Shinran, Yeshua and Dogen

Yagi sees an extraordinary similarity between the great theologian of the cosmic Christ, Paul, and the great theologian of the cosmic Amida, Shinran (1173–1262), both of which figures are like the spirit of the Infinite who works in every person and in all beings, "uttering ineffable groans until all the world be saved," as Paul described, and swearing not to enter nirvana until all have been brought to the Pure Land, as Shinran reported.[68] For Paul and Shinran both Christ and Amida are divine, not in se—that is, as the Father and dharmakaya—but as the Ineffable ad extra.

Yagi likewise sees a great similarity in the teaching and kind of language used by Yeshua and the pioneer Japanese Zen teacher Dogen (1200–1253) and the modern Japanese Zen teacher Hisamatsu (1889–1980). He finds that Yeshua, Dogen, and Hisamatsu speak "from within Ultimate Reality, from things as 'they really are.'" Thus, Yagi believes, "one can rightly understand the 'I Am' statements of Jesus found in the Gospel of John, as also statements of Dogen and Hisamatsu that seem either spiritually presumptuous or heedless of common human experience. That is, both Jesus and Dogen (Zen) said 'I' from the level of the Transcendent." Both taught that authentic human life begins with oneself—love of oneself, and self-awareness—but moves out through the Reign of God, through dharma, the ultimate working force of the cosmos. "Only the dharma that works within us is Ultimate Reality. … as with Jesus, we are to lose the self on one level … to find it again at a higher level, the level of harmonious, cooperative relationship with the Most High and with the Whole, of which S/he is the Source. Relationship is the primary reality."[69]

Yagi's Place in Japanese Christianity

Seiichi Yagi was born in 1932 in Yokohama in a Christian family, studied Western classics and philosophy at Tokyo University, New Testament at the Graduate School of the same and with Ernst Käsemann at the University of Göttingen, receiving a Doctor of Humane Letters from the University of Kyushu in 1962. Although he has taught Christian theology part-time at various European and Japanese universities, no Japanese department of theology has ever invited him to teach. Consequently, he has taught German at the Tokyo University of Engineering for more than twenty-two years, and only in 1988 began to teach philosophy and ethics at a newly founded university, Toin University of Yokohama.

Richard Drummond speaks of Yagi's potential leadership among Japanese Christians being somewhat hindered by his "inability in recent years to believe in the specifically redemptive aspects of Jesus' life, death, and resurrection,"[70] which of course is another way of speaking of the Christian doctrine of the atonement. However, just how Yeshua's life and death could lead to the salvation of other human beings has been variously understood in Christian history. The now traditional understanding by way of atonement, in a rather crassly materialistic, even juridical, manner, in fact was developed only in the tenth century by Anselm of Canterbury in his famous work *Cur Deus Homo*? But surely the more exemplary model of understanding as put forward especially in the Reformed tradition, but elsewhere as well, is also quite congruent with the biblical tradition, and certainly with the self-understanding of Yeshua that we are able to glean from pages of the gospels.[71]

Another Japanese Christian, Yasuo Furuya, who is very sympathetic to Yagi's work, also remarks that partly because of Yagi's untraditional approach and partly because of the partially continuing Japanese theological conservatism, Yagi has been largely isolated from the rest of the Christian theological world—though Furuya himself is working hard to overcome that isolation.[72]

Though Yagi is thus yet another example of a prophet not being accepted by his own, at the same time the well-known Swiss Protestant New Testament scholar, Ulrich Luz, recently wrote that, "Yagi is one of the most significant writers of Japan. His numerous books are sometimes printed in editions of six figures and are read by scores of thousands, perhaps indeed by hundreds of thousands … mostly non-Christians."[73]

Two "Conversions"

In his youthful studies Yagi underwent two important "conversion" experiences. One was the study of the New Testament, first in Japan and then with Ernst Käsemann in Germany. The second also occurred in Germany, where through study he also began to discover his "native" Buddhism. He describes this second conversion experience, which occurred while reading in a train in Germany a Buddhist writing entitled, "Open Wideness—Nothing of the Holy":

> The train fortunately was empty. I could find a place in a corner and give myself over undisturbed to my reading. I read with such a zeal and concentration that eventually I became weary. Exhausted and

> relaxed I looked out at the countryside near Kassel. The rain had just stopped; the clouds separated. The opening in the clouds widened so that the blue sky was visible. Suddenly there flashed in me the words: "Open Wideness—Nothing of the Holy." I stood up and looked around. Something had happened to me which I could not immediately grasp. Every single thing I saw looked completely different from the way it looked before, although it had indeed remained the same. The first thing I said to myself was this: "I have understood the tree to be a tree. How wrong that was!" What I thought was the tree was in reality only the commonly held concept "tree." Without being aware of it, I had projected the commonly held concept into the "object," and when I looked at it I drew out of it only that which I had previously projected into it, and called that "perceiving an object." I perceived only what I had already long known. That, however, was not seeing, was not an encounter with the being. Now, however, I saw the "tree," as it presented itself from itself, before all forming of concepts.[74]

Ulrich Luz notes that Yagi saw a parallelism, indeed a congruence, between these two "conversions." Yagi learned in Christianity what it means to lose oneself in order to receive the gift of a new, deeper self, no longer, as he would put it later, the "mere Ego," but the fully authentic "Self," so that Paul's statement became of central importance for him: "I live now not I but Christ lives in me"; in Christianity Yagi also learned liberation from the "letter of the law" (moralism). In Buddhism Yagi experienced the gift of liberation from the toils of objectifying language in general. He learned to perceive below the level of the "discriminating intellect," as he named it, which necessarily perceived and spoke of things as distinct and separate (in separate substance categories), the level of relationality whereby all things can in fact exist only in intimate, existence-constituting relationship with each other.

Yagi himself stated it thus: "In both events [his two "conversions"] I was freed from the constant process of being myself shaped by language. It was just that the first (Christian) focused on acting and the second (Buddhist) focused on seeing." He then, particularly as a Protestant Christian, went on to comment on his perception of the heart of Christian faith: "Does not the essence of Christian faith lie in the liberation from conceptual language more than in the justification of the godless?[75] Most recently Yagi commented:

Thus, based on this parallelism, I have been trying, not only as a New Testament student, but as a writer, to show that the formation of New Testament thinking, inclusive of its earliest kerygma, can be explained as the interpretation of the event of "Enlightenment" (2 Cor 4: 6) which took place in the disciples of Jesus after his death, without any presupposition of a "supernatural" intervention by God into history. That was already the theme of my first book, The Formation of New Testament Thinking, 1963.[76]

This Book as a Bridge

Buddhism, especially Zen Buddhism, often insists that its key insights cannot be understood with the intellect, but must be experienced. Nevertheless, many Buddhists try endlessly to explain Buddhism with their intellects and language—in my experience, very often in an unclear, confusing manner. Of course, the quality of knowledge resulting from a rational analysis on the one hand and immediate intuition on the other is different. Nevertheless, each dimension of reality can be known, and hence articulated, through both cognitive methods, though of course with correspondingly varying results. Hence, it will just not do to fall back on the old dodge: "This is too deep to explain"; "this is a mystery"; or, as Gregory the Great put it fourteen centuries ago: "This is not a lie, but a mystery," Non mendacium sed mysterium. Thinking, both discursively and intuitively, and speaking accordingly are at the very core of being human.

If Buddhism has an insight into the core of being human, it must be possible to grasp it with the discursive intellect in a manner proportionate to it and express it in language. Of course, the categories in which it is grasped and expressed will have to be appropriate to the insight (e.g., process rather than substance categories). It is precisely this appropriateness that has so very often been lacking—and that is what Seiichi Yagi in this book, and elsewhere, begins so lucidly to supply. He begins to cast key Buddhist ways of understanding and describing reality in discursive thought categories and language that are quite understandable not only by someone brought up in a Buddhist thought world, nor even just someone brought up in the Western thought world, but by both, and I believe even beyond. He is forging here both a new commonly human consciousness and corresponding language, which I have elsewhere called "Ecumenical Esperanto."[77]

In this book Yagi sees "dependent co-origination," *pratītyasamutpāda*, and emptiness, sunyata, as at the heart of Buddhist thinking. All reality is ultimately and intimately relational and in process. However, this understanding of reality is not how the world is presented to us in our common sense, everyday perception of things, and if it were, we, both individually and communally, would collapse in chaos and anarchy. Rather, we normally understand the world as made up of distinct, self-subsisting substances, and hence we are able to put things in rational order according to various rules or laws. This manner of thinking Yagi refers to as flowing from our "differentiating intellect," and he of course in no way denigrates it; in fact, he uses it very effectively in this book to explain it and its contrary counterpart, which might be called the "integrating intellect."

It is by means of the "Front-Structure" that Yagi explains in clear, understandable fashion how all reality must in fact be relational, how totally independent, self-subsisting entities cannot in reality exist. Through this conceptual instrument he makes apparent to the "differentiating intellect" how it is that the "integrating intellect" has grasped intuitively the insight that the world is *pratītyasamutpāda*, sunyata, that is, is relational, processive.

By its very nature, this is very abstract stuff, and hence difficult to explain rationally. That is why Buddhists have tended to move to paradoxical language in an attempt to communicate it—but, in my judgment, with only limited success, for paradoxical language is a rather blunt instrument, suitable for its shock value, but hardly suitable for clear explanation. Yagi, however, avoids the difficulties connected with paradoxical language by brilliantly (quite literally) employing explanatory analogies with concrete examples. One set of analogies is spatial; another is tonal, concentrating especially on music.

Another key Buddhist concept for Yagi is the "No-Self," Anatta teaching. Although Yagi does not refer to it much by name in this book, he nevertheless sets his interpretation of it forth in very careful fashion when he makes a distinction between what he calls the "mere Ego," which is a rather surface dimension of the human being, paralleling the differentiating intellect, and the Self (with an upper-case "S"), paralleling the authentic relational, processive self (which he describes in polar fashion), however it is described by various terms in the differing strands of Buddhism.

Different from a number of Western interpreters of Buddhism, Yagi sees the Transcendent in the Buddhism of all periods. Initially this might surprise not only some Westerners but even some Buddhists, but I suspect that this surprise, and perhaps skepticism, will fade as they read how he explains the Transcendent. Two analogies are used prominently here, namely, the Transcendent as a "Field of Force," within which individual beings exist and act, and as a pervasive life force which permeates all reality, giving it its very relationality and processive character.

After laying out these and other basic ways of Buddhist thinking in categories and with analogies that make them understandable to Westerners, and others, Yagi proceeds explicitly to lay out some of the specifically Christian—actually, Judeo-Christian—insights which more or less correspond to the Buddhist. He sees the Buddhist "integrative" approach embodied in the Judeo-Christian perception that at the core of being human is love (the two great commandments of love which incorporate all the others—or, "Love, and do what you will," Ama, et fac quod vis, as Augustine put it). Here Yagi finds that the Judeo-Christian tradition has been more consistently implementive of the "integrative," the "communal," dimension of the relational, the *pratītyasamutpāda*, human life, than has Buddhism. True, there are the notions of Karuna, compassion, and the Bodhisattva in the Buddhist tradition, but Yagi suggests that Buddhism has tended to be too individualistic—one might say that this is especially true of Pure Land and Zen Buddhism, though not of Nichiren. But this is a matter of balance, not essence, and of course the whole point of dialogue is for the two partners to learn from each other.

Within the context of the conceptual analysis in this book, Yagi also carefully makes the distinction, which many other Christian theologians have also made on other grounds, between the concrete historical person Jesus, Yeshua, the spiritualized Christ as the Logos incarnate and the Logos itself as the force operating within individual humans, and indeed in the whole of reality. In the process, he makes use of the distinction drawn by his fellow Christian, Katsumi Takizawa (which is like that of the medieval Japanese Zen thinker, Dogen), between the primary contact with Ultimate Reality, which is present in all beings, and the secondary contact, which is the consciousness of the primary contact—which the Buddhists call Enlightenment. He sees this distinction in Yeshua in preeminent fashion in the sense that what made Yeshua so extraordinary was his profoundly pervasive secondary contact.

Such a Christological understanding, however, means that Christianity (and Buddhism) cannot make claims of absoluteness, in the sense of being the sole means of reaching Ultimate Reality, of attaining Salus hol(i)ness. Hence, both can learn from each other. But to do so, each must walk the bridge of dialogue to reach the other. And Seiichi Yagi has here helped to build such a bridge. Let's take a walk.

Endnotes

[1] By religion here I understand "an explanation of the meaning of life, and how to live accordingly." Religions customarily have the four "Cs": Creed, Code, Cult, Community-structure; and are ultimately based on some understanding of the Transcendent, that is, an ultimate reality that "goes-beyond" our everyday experience of life. An ideology, e.g., atheistic humanism or Marxism, functions basically the same as a religion for its followers, but is not ultimately based on some understanding of the Transcendent, at least not in its usual meaning.

[2] Leonard Swidler, "The Dialogue Decalogue: Ground Rules for Interreligious Dialogue," *Journal of Ecumenical Studies* 20, no. 1 (Winter 1983): pp. 1–4. These guidelines have been reprinted in more than thirty other periodicals and books, including in German, Portuguese, Hungarian, Polish, Swedish, Arabic, Chinese, Japanese, and Korean.

[3] See, e.g., J. Edgar Bruns, *The Christian Buddhism of St. John* (Paulist Press, 1971).

[4] See Wilfred Cantwell Smith, *Towards a World Theology* (Westminster Press, 1981), pp. 7–11.

[5] John Berthrong, "Third North American Buddhist-Christian Theological Encounter," *Journal of Ecumenical Studies* 23, no. 4 (Fall 1986): pp. 775f.

[6] Daniel J. O'Hanlon, "Third International Buddhist-Christian Conference," *Journal of Ecumenical Studies* 24, no. 3 (Summer 1987):, pp. 513f.

[7] The Society for Buddhist-Christian Studies, in addition to making the *Buddhist-Christian Studies* its journal to carry substantive articles, also launched a *Newsletter* at the Graduate Theological Union. It is from its first number, Spring 1988, that most of the information in this section is garnered.

[8] See, for example, the report by James Conner, "Fifth Buddhist-Christ Meditation Conference at Naropa," *Journal of Ecumenical Studies* 22, no. 4 (Fall 1985):, pp. 879f., which was attended by over 200 people.

[9] Cromwell Crawford, "The Buddha's Thoughts on Thinking: Implications for Ecumenical Dialogue," *Journal of Ecumenical Studies* 21, no. 2 (Spring 1984): p. 242, noted that "the Buddha saw things in their uniqueness, but this did not incur any fragmentation in his thinking. The part was part, but it was part of the whole. … This means that interrelationship belongs to the essential nature of things."

The Buddhist scholar David Kalupahana, *Buddhist Philosophy* (University Press of Hawaii, 1976), p. 29, comments on Gautama's statement of the principle of *pratītyasamutpāda*: "If this is, that comes to be; from the arising of this that arises." *The Middle Length Sayings*, trans. I.B. Horner (Pali Text Society, 1967), I.262–263; vol. 1, p. 319, states as follows: "This statement, found in many places in the early texts, explains the conception of causality or causal uniformity which the Buddha arrived at after a perusal of the various instances of causal happenings and which came to be known as the golden mean between the two extremes, eternalism and annihilationism. It is, indeed, the truth about the world which the Buddha claimed he discovered and which became the 'central' doctrine of Buddhism. It was the Buddha's answer to both the eternalist theory of the Substantialists, who posited an unchanging immutable 'self' (*atman*), and the annihilationist theory of the non-Substantialists, who denied continuity altogether."

[10] Paul O. Ingram, "Buddhist and Christian Paradigms of Selfhood," (paper presented at conference on "Paradigm Shift in Buddhism and Christianity: Cultural Systems and the Self," Honolulu, HI January 3–11 1984), p. 37.

[11] Masao Abe, "A Dynamic Unity in Religious Pluralism: A Proposal from the Buddhist Point of View," in *The Experience of Religious Diversity*, ed. John Hick and Hasan Askari (Gower, 1985), pp. 163–190.

[12] John Hick, "Religious Diversity as Challenge and Promise," ibid., p. 19.

[13] Abe, "Dynamic Unity," p. 184.

[14] Santosh Chandra Sengupta, "The Misunderstanding of Hinduism," in *Truth and Dialogue in World Religions: Conflicting Truth Claims,* ed. John Hick (Westminster Press, 1974) p. 97.

[15] Tang Yi, "Taoism as a Living Philosophy," *Journal of Chinese Philosophy* 12, no. 4 (December 1985): p. 408.

[16] See, Leonard Swidler, "God, Father and Mother," in *The Bible Today*, September, 1984, pp. 300–305.

[17] Jung Young Lee, "Can God be Change Itself?" *Journal of Ecumenical Studies* 10, no. 4 (Fall 1973), pp. 752–770.

[18] Jay McDaniel, "The God of the Oppressed and the God Who is Empty," *Journal of Ecumenical Studies* 23, no. 3 (Fall 1985): p. 687.

[19] Pope Paul VI, cited in "Charter of the Rights of Catholics in the Church," in *A Catholic Bill of Rights,* ed. Leonard Swidler and Herbert Brien (Sheed & Ward, 1988), p. 2.

[20] See, for example, my *Yeshua: A Model for Moderns* (Sheed & Ward, 1988); and *Dialogue: The Way Forward* (Fortress Press, 1989).

[21] See Charles T. Waldrop, "Karl Barth and Pure Land Buddhism," *Journal of Ecumenical Studies* 24, no. 4 (Fall 1987), pp. 574–597. Waldrop undertakes a very gentle engagement with Barth's rather harshly dismissive treatment of Pure Land Buddhism, as well as all other religions, and concludes: "We can learn a great deal from Barth's treatment of Pure Land Buddhism that will help us engage profitably in interfaith dialogue within the context of Christian systematic theology. However, the foundation that Barth has provided also stimulates us to go beyond Barth." (p. 597)

[22] Lecture at the University of Tübingen, June, 1985, by Dr. Sulak Sivaraksa, and personal conversations with him in Bangkok, January, 1989. See also his books: *An Engaged Buddhism; A Buddhist Vision for Renewing Society; Siamese Resurgence* and particularly his *Religion and Development* (Payap College, 1981), partly for which he was tried on the charge of *lèse majesté.*

[23] Buddhadasa Bhikkhu, *Dhammic Socialism*, trans. and ed. Donald K. Swearer (Thai Inter-Religious Commission for Development, 1986).

[24] Donald K. Swearer, "The Vision of Bhikkhu Buddhadasa," in ibid., p. 31.

[25] Ibid., pp. 32f.

[26] See, for example, his book *Looking to America to Solve Thailand's Problems* (Thai America Project, 1987).

[27] Ibid., p. 64. Rajavaramuni has a strong commitment to critical-thinking education, to freedom, and to democracy: "In developing a democratic society, we must have this freedom of intellect … Buddhism requires this kind of intellect. If we cannot develop people to the point of having freedom of intellect, there is no way that the development of democracy will succeed." (p. 81)

[28] Aloysius Pieris, SJ, "The Buddha and the Christ: Mediators of Liberation," in *The Myth of Christian Uniqueness: Toward a Pluralistic Theology of Religions*, ed. John Hick and Paul F. Knitter (Orbis, 1987), p. 168.

[29] Dayar Powar, "Siddhartha," *Panchasheel*, (October, 1972), p. 7, translated into English and quoted in JB Gokhale-Turner, "*Bhakti* or *Vidroha*: Continuity and Change in Dalit Sahitya," *Journal of African and Asian Studies* 15, no. 1–2 (January 1980): p. 38.

[30] Pieris, "The Buddha and the Christ," p. 169.

[31] See, "Jesus Was a Feminist," *Catholic World*, January, 1971, pp. 171–183, was reprinted over thirty times in many countries and translated in seven languages. See also a fuller treatment in my *Biblical Affirmations of Woman*, (Westminster Press, 1979), and in my *Yeshua: A Model for Moderns* (Sheed & Ward, 1988).

[32] See Leonard Swidler, *Biblical Affirmations of Women*, pp. 290–338.

[33] See the discussion "Is It True that the Buddha Never Wanted Women in the Sangha?" by Chatsumarn Kabilsingh et al. in *Newsletter on International Buddhist Women's Activities* 18 (January–March, 1989): pp. 5–24, where the argument is in favor of ordaining Buddhist women today.

[34] One of the obvious leaders is the Buddhism woman scholar Dr. Chatsumarn Kabilsingh of Thammasat University, Bangkok, Thailand, who has published many articles and books in the area and has started her own newsletter. See ibid.

[35] Olivier Chegaray Mep, "Die Verkündigung des Evangeliums in Japan," *Die Katholische Mission* 107, no. 6 (November/December 1988): p. 194, "The Church very effectively through the 'Committee for Justice and Peace' takes a stand against every kind of injustice: against the testing of nuclear weapons in the Pacific, against the oppressive power of huge firms, against practices of multi-nationals in Southeast Asia, against political suppression in Korea and the Philippines, and for genuine solidarity among the peoples of Asia." The author is a French missionary in Japan and this article is an abbreviated version of his article in *Église et Mission*, December, 1987.

[36] *The Canonical Textbook of Won Buddhism*, trans. Pal-Khn Chon (Won Buddhist Publications, 1971), p. 366.

[37] *United Religions* (Iri City, Korea, 1981).

[38] I have Frank E. Reynolds to thank for this grouping of the major Chinese (Japanese) Buddhist schools into "catholic" and "protestant." Niels C. Nielsen, Jr., et al., *Religions of the World*, 2nd ed. (New York: St. Martins Press, 2nd ed., 1988), pp. 244ff.

[39] Richard C. Bush, et al., *The Religious World*, 2nd ed. (Macmillan, 2nd ed., 1988), p. 143.

[40] *Nihongi, The Chronicles of Japan from the Earliest Times to 697 A.D.*, trans. Charles E. Tuttle Co., 1972), pp. 10–12.

[41] Quoted in Clarence H. Hamilton, ed., *Buddhism: A Religion of Infinite Compassion* (The Liberal Arts Press, 1952), p. 145.

[42] Cited in M. Anesaki, *History of Japanese Religion* (Honpa Hongwanji Mission of Hawaii, 1955), p. 267.

[43] Shinshu Seiten, *The Holy Scriptures of Shinshu* (Honpa Hongwanji Mission of Hawaii, 1955), p. 267.

[44] Bush et al., *The Religious World*, p. 154.

[45] Joseph Kitagawa, *Religion in Japanese History* (Columbia University Press, 1966), p. 296, speaks of over sixteen million family units.

[46] John A. Hutchison, *Paths of Faith*, 2nd ed. (McGraw-Hill, 1975), pp. 284f.

[47] Ibid., p. 287.

[48] Mep, "Die Verkündigung," p. 194.

[49] In this section I am especially indebted to Ernest D. Piryns, "Japanese Theology and Inculturation," *Journal of Ecumenical Studies* 24, no. 4 (Fall 1987): pp. 535–556.

[50] See Richard Drummond, "The Non-Church Movement in Japan," *Journal of Ecumenical Studies* 2, no. 3 (Fall 1965): pp. 448–451; Akio Dohi, "The Historical Development of the Non-Church Movement in Japan," *Journal of Ecumenical Studies* 2, no. 3 (Fall 1965): pp. 452–468; Carlo Caldarola, "Japanese Reaction to the Institutional Church," *Journal of Ecumenical Studies* 9, no. 3 (Summer 1972):, pp. 489–520. The last is heavily based on sociological field research.

[51] Still in 1972 Carlo Caldarola, "Japanese Reaction," p. 500, could write: "Barth has been a kind of theological pope in the Japanese Protestant Church for a long time. … Barth seems to be still more influential than any other theologian. All of his writings have been translated into Japanese and still are among the best sellers of theological publications in the country."

[52] English translation (SCM Press, 1951).

[53] *Bukkyō to Kirisutokyō* [Buddhism and Christianity] (Hozokan, 1964).

[54] See Silvio Fittipaldi, "The Encounter Between Roman Catholicism and Zen Buddhism From a Roman Catholic Point of View," (PhD diss. Temple University, 1976) for an analysis of the writings of many of these "dialogic" theologians.

[55] Cf. Yōji Inoue, *Nihon to Iesu no Kao* [Japan and the Face of Jesus] (Hokuyosha,: 1976), and Yōji Inoue, "Western Christianity and Japan," *The Japan Missionary Bulletin* 35 (May 1981): pp. 223–227.

[56] See, e.g., Yōji Inoue, "Miura Ayako and Her World," trans. Stephen Luttio, *The Japan Christian Quarterly* 51 (Spring 1985): pp. 96–102.

[57] Piryns, "Japanese Theology," p. 548.

[58] Ibid., p. 543.

[59] Richard H. Drummond, "Dialogue and Integration: The Theological Challenge of Yagi Seiichi," *Journal of Ecumenical Studies* 24, no. 4 (Fall 1987): p. 563.

[60] Ibid., p. 571.

[61] Ira Progoff, *The Practice of Process Meditation* (Dialogue House Library 1980).

[62] Quoted in Drummond, "Dialogue and Integration," p. 571.

[63] Ibid., p. 560.

[64] Ibid., p. 572.

[65] Seiichi Yagi, "Buddhism and Christianity: a dialogue with John B. Cobb, Jr.," *The Northeast Asia Journal of Theology* 20–21 (March/September 1978): p. 7, cited in Drummond, ibid., p. 60.

[66] John Hick, "Rethinking Christian Doctrine in the Light of Religious Pluralism," in *IRF: A Newsletter of the International Religious Foundation, Inc.* 3, no. 4 (Fall 1988): p. 2. This is only the most recent publication at the time of writing in which Hick has expressed this notion.

[67] Hick, "Rethinking Christian Doctrine," p. 5.

[68] See Seiichi Yagi, *Pauro, Shinran, Iesu, Zen* [Paul and Shinran; Jesus and Zen] (Hozokan, 1983) in Paul O. Ingram and Frederick J. Streng, eds., *Buddhist-Christian Dialogue: Mutual Renewal and Transformation* (University of Hawaii Press, 1986); and "*Paulus und Shinran,*" *Evangelische Theologie* 48, no. 1 (1988): pp. 36–46.

[69] Drummond, "Dialogue and Integration," pp. 569f.

[70] Ibid., p. 562.

[71] See as one modern attempt in this mode my *Yeshua: A Model for Moderns*, where it is argued that Yeshua "saves" by the model of how to live an authentic human life through what he "thought, taught and wrought."

[72] Yasua Furuya, *Shukyo no Shingaku* [A Theology of Religions] (Yordansha, 1985), p. 327 and passim.

[73] Ulrich Luz, "Zur Einführung," in Seiichi Yagi, *Die Front-Struktur*, p. 10.

[74] An autobiographical sketch as reported in Luz, "Einführung," pp. 11f.

[75] Ibid., p. 12.

[76] Note to Leonard Swidler, January 27, 1989.

[77] See Leonard Swidler, "Interreligious and Interideological Dialogue: The Matrix for All Systematic Reflection Today," Leonard Swidler, ed., *Toward a Universal Theology of Religion* (Orbis Books, 1987), pp. 5–50.

Selected Bibliography

Abe, Masao. "A Dynamic Unity in Religious Pluralism: A Proposal from the Buddhist Point of View." In *The Experience of Religious Diversity,* edited by John Hick and Hasan Askari. Gower, 1985.

Anesaki, M. *History of Japanese Religion.* Honpa Hongwanji Mission of Hawaii, 1955.

Aston, WG, translator. *Nihongi: Chronicles of Japan from the Earliest Times to A.D 697.* Charles E. Tuttle Company, 1972.

Berthrong, John. "Third North American Buddhist-Christian Theological Encounter." *Journal of Ecumenical Studies* 23, no. 4 (1986): 775–776.

Bhikkhu, Buddhadasa. *Dhammic Socialism.* Translated and edited by Donald K. Swearer. Thai Inter-Religious Commission for Development, 1986.

Brien, Herbert and Leonard Swidler, editors. "Charter of the Rights of Catholics in the Church." *A Catholic Bill of Rights.* Sheed & Ward, 1988.

Bruns, J. Edgar. *The Christian Buddhism of St. John.* Paulist Press, 1971.

Bush, Richard C., et. al. *The Religious World.* 2nd ed. Macmillan, 1988.

Caldorala, Carlo. "Japanese Reaction to the Institutional Church." *Journal of Ecumenical Studies* 9, no. 3 (1972): 489–520.

Conner, James. "Fifth Buddhist-Christ Meditation Conference at Naropa." *Journal of Ecumenical Studies* 22, no. 4 (1985): 879–880.

Crawford, Cromwell. "The Buddha's Thoughts on Thinking: Implications for Ecumenical Dialogue." *Journal of Ecumenical Studies* 21, no. 2 (1984): 24.

Dohi, Akio. "The Historical Development of the Non-Church Movement in Japan." *Journal of Ecumenical Studies* 2, no. 3 (1965): 452–468.

Drummond, Richard. "Dialogue and Integration: The Theological Challenge of Yagi Seiichi." *Journal of Ecumenical Studies* 24, no. 4 (1987): 563.

Drummond, Richard. "The Non-Church Movement in Japan." *Journal of Ecumenical Studies* 2, no. 3 (1965): 448–451.

Fittipaldi, Silvio. "The Encounter Between Roman Catholicism and Zen Buddhism From a Roman Catholic Point of View." PhD diss., Temple University, 1976.

Furuya, Yasua. *Shukyo no Shingaku* [A Theology of Religions]. Yordansha, 1985.

Hamilton, Clarence H. ed. *Buddhism: A Religion of Infinite Compassion.* The Liberal Arts Press, 1952.

Hick, John. "Religious Diversity as Challenge and Promise." In *The Experience of Religious Diversity,* edited by John Hick and Hasan Askari. Gower, 1985.

Hick, John. "Rethinking Christian Doctrine in the Light of Religious Pluralism." *IRF: A Newsletter of the International Religious Foundation, Inc.* 3, no. 4 (1988): 2.

Horner, IB, translator. *The Middle Length Sayings.* I.262–263, vol. 1. Pali Text Society, 1967.

Hutchison, John A. *Paths of Faith,* 2nd ed. McGraw-Hill, 1975.

Ingram, Paul O. "Buddhist and Christian Paradigms of Selfhood." Paper presented at the Paradigm Shift in Buddhism and Christianity: Cultural Systems and the Self conference, Honolulu, HI January 3–11, 1984.

Inoue, Yōji. "Miura Ayako and Her World." Translated by Stephen Luttio. *The Japan Christian Quarterly* 51 (1985): 96–102.

Inoue, Yōji. *Nihon to Iesu no Kao* [Japan and the Face of Jesus]. Hokuyosha, 1976.

Inoue, Yōji. "Western Christianity and Japan." *The Japan Missionary Bulletin* 35 (1981): 223–227.

Kabilsingh, Chatsumarn et. al. "Is it True that the Buddha Never Wanted Women in the Sangha?" *Newsletter on International Buddhist Women's Activities* 18 (1989).

Kalupahana, David. *Buddhist Philosophy.* University Press of Hawaii, 1976.

Kitagawa, Joseph. *Religion in Japanese History.* Columbia University Press, 1966.

Kitamori, Kazoh. *Theology of the Pain of God.* SCM Press, 1951.

Kyojuno, Won Pulkyo. *The Canonical Textbook of Won Buddhism.* Translated by Pal-Khn Chon. Won Buddhist Publications, 1971.

Lee, Jung Young. "Can God Be Change Itself?" *Journal of Ecumenical Studies* 10, no. 4 (1973): 752–770.

Luz, Ulrich. Introduction to *Die Front-Struktur.* Chr. Kaiser Verlag, 1988.

McDaniel, Jay. "The God of the Oppressed and the God Who Is Empty." *Journal of Ecumenical Studies* 23, no. 3 (1985): 687.

Mep, Olivier Chegaray. "Die Verkündigung des Evangeliums in Japan." *Die Katholische Mission* 107, no. 6 (1988): 194.

Nielsen, Niels C., Jr., et. al. *Religions of the World.* 2nd ed. Macmillan, 1988.

O'Hanlon, Daniel J. "Third International Buddhist-Christian Conference." *Journal of Ecumenical Studies* 24, no. 3 (1987): 513–514.

Phra Rajavaramuni. *Looking to America to Solve Thailand's Problems.* Translated by Grant A. Olson. The Thai-American Project, 1987.

Pieris, Aloysius, SJ. "The Buddha and the Christ: Mediators of Liberation." In *The Myth of Christian Uniqueness: Toward a Pluralistic Theology of Religions,* edited by John Hick and Paul F. Knitter. Orbis, 1987.

Piryns, Ernest D. "Japanese Theology and Inculturation." *Journal of Ecumenical Studies* 24, no. 4 (1987): 535–556.

Seiten, Shinshu. *The Holy Scriptures of Shinshu.* Honpa Hongwanji Mission of Hawaii, 1955.

Sengupta, Santosh Chandra. "The Misunderstanding of Hinduism." In *Truth and Dialogue in World Religions: Conflicting Truth Claims,* edited by John Hick. Westminster Press, 1974.

Sivaraksa, Sulak. *A Buddhist Vision for Renewing Society.* Thianwan Publishing, 1986.

Sivaraksa, Sulak. *Religion and Development.* Thai Inter-Religious Commission for Development, 1987.

Sivaraksa, Sulak. *Siamese Resurgence.* Asian Cultural Forum on Development, 1985.

Sivaraksa, Sulak. *A Socially Engaged Buddhism.* Thai Inter-Religious Commission for Development, 1987.

Smith, Wilfred Cantwell. *Towards a World Theology.* Westminster Press, 1981.

Swidler, Leonard. *Biblical Affirmations of Woman.* Westminster Press, 1979.

Swidler, Leonard. "The Dialogue Decalogue: Ground Rules for Interreligious Dialogue." *Journal of Ecumenical Studies* 20, no. 1 (1983): 1–4.

Swidler, Leonard. *Dialogue: The Way Forward.* Fortress Press, 1989.

Swidler, Leonard. "God, Father and Mother." *The Bible Today* (1984): 300–305.

Swidler, Leonard. "Interreligious and Interideological Dialogue: The Matrix for All Systematic Reflection Today." In *Toward a Universal Theology of Religion,* edited by Leonard Swidler. Orbis Books, 1987.

Swidler, Leonard. "Jesus Was a Feminist." *Catholic World* (1971): 177–183.

Swidler, Leonard. *Yeshua: A Model for Moderns.* Sheed & Ward, 1988.

Takizawa, Katsumi. *Bukkyō to Kirisutokyō* [Buddhism and Christianity]. Hozokan, 1964.

Turner, JB Gokhale. "Bhakti or Vidroha: Continuity and Change in Dalit Sahitya." *Journal of African and Asian Studies* 15, no. 1–2 (1980): 38.

Waldrop, Charles T. "Karl Barth and Pure Land Buddhism." *Journal of Ecumenical Studies* 24, no. 4 (1987): 574–597.

Yagi, Seiichi. "Buddhism and Christianity: a dialogue with John B. Cobb, Jr." *The Northeast Asia Journal of Theology* 20–21 (1978): 7.

Yagi, Seiichi. "Paulus und Shinran." *Evangelische Theologie* 48, no. 1 (1988): 36–46.

Yagi, Seiichi. "Pauro, Shinran, Iesu, Zen," [Paul and Shinran; Jesus and Zen]. In *Buddhist-Christian Dialogue: Mutual Renewal and Transformation,* edited by Paul O. Ingram and Frederick J. Steng. University of Hawaii Press, 1986.

Yi, Tang. "Taoism as a Living Philosophy." *Journal of Chinese Philosophy* 12, no. 4 (1985): 408.

About the Authors

Dr. Leonard Swidler is the founder and president of the Dialogue Institute and a recently retired professor of Temple University's Department of Religion where he taught for 56 years. At Temple and as a visiting professor at many universities around the world, he has mentored a generation of US and international scholars in the work of interreligious dialogue.

He has proposed a "Universal Declaration of a Global Ethic," based on various religious and ethical communities, ethical groups, and geographical religions, encouraging work and discussion in drafting their own versions of a global ethic.

Professor Swidler is the author of more than 100 books, including *The Power of Dialogue*; *Jewish–Christian–Muslim Agreement and Collaboration; Authentic Humanity*; and *Jesus Was a Feminist.*

Dr. Seiichi Yagi is a prominent voice in philosophical foundations of interreligious thought and a major representative of Buddhist-Christian dialogue worldwide. Now professor emeritus at the Tokyo Institute of Technology and the University of Yokohama, he has taught Philosophical and Religious Thought at a number of universities across Japan. An active supporter of the Japan Society for Buddhist-Christian Studies, Professor Yagi's work has been instrumental in expanding interfaith literature and interreligious thought in Japan, Germany, and the US.

Yagi's work proposes a philosophy of religion blending Buddhist and Christian thought into the singular idea that religion overcomes an ego-centered existence to realize a truer, deeper Self. His work on Front-Structures have been integral to furthering this philosophy.

Professor Yagi is the author of more than 20 influential publications in multiple languages which have been praised by scholars worldwide.

About iPub Cloud International

iPub Cloud International is a 501(c)(3) nonprofit publishing house dedicated to elevating the voices of the disenfranchised, marginalized, and those unable to afford the high costs of traditional publishing. As a women-owned and women-led organization, we also take immense pride in having individuals with disabilities in senior leadership roles, reflecting our mission of inclusivity and empowerment.

We are not just a publisher; we are a champion for change, seeking to amplify stories that matter. By fostering a culture of enlightenment and progress, we empower voices that inspire action, provoke thought, and pave the way for a more compassionate and understanding world. Our work touches lives—not only through the authors, contributors, and team members who make it possible but also through the readers and communities who engage with the transformative ideas we bring to light. At iPub Cloud International, every book, story, and idea we publish is a step toward building a brighter, more inclusive future.

iPub Cloud International
Poughkeepsie, NY 12603
Visit our website to stay up to date on your favorite writers and subscribe for news on new releases, events, and promotions:
www.iPubCloud.org
Join the conversation at iPubForum.com

www.ingramcontent.com/pod-product-compliance
Lightning Source LLC
Chambersburg PA
CBHW050654270326
41927CB00012B/3027

* 9 7 8 1 9 4 8 5 7 5 9 5 9 *